Les Ey
de-Tayac
and the Vézère Valley

Jean-Claude Blanchet
Inspecteur général de l'Archéologie
Jean-Jacques Cleyet-Merle
Director, Musée national de Préhistoire

The Vézère Valley, with its dense concentration of amazingly well-preserved archaeological sites between Montignac and Les Eyzies, is the place where Franco-Cantabrian Palaeolithic art was first recognised. After some 150 years of practically uninterrupted excavations and research, these sites remain of such scientific importance that in 1979 UNESCO placed about fifteen of them on the World Heritage List. Although *Australopithecus* do not seem to have roamed the region, it was the adopted home of *Homo sapiens*—Neanderthal and Cro-Magnon man. Our ancestors soon came to enjoy a special environment where numerous caves and natural shelters could be found at the foot of the tall limestone cliffs and favourable climatic conditions prevailed. The Vézère Valley was never a frozen desert, even at the height of the ice age: a thin strip of vegetation provided the inhabitants with a supply of game, fish, wood for heating, and, of course, flint, indispensable for making tools and arms.

While the cave of Lascaux immediately springs to mind, other sites have helped improve our knowledge about our distant past. The Musée national de Préhistoire at Les Eyzies, the nerve centre and obligatory point of passage through the "Valley of Mankind", helps us understand it better.

The village and museum, Les Eyzies-de-Tayac.

The history of prehistoric archaeology

From the origins to modern prehistory

Stratigraphy:
A succession of archaeological deposits, or layers (strata), normally providing a relative chronological sequence with the earliest at the bottom; it is one of the major tools of archaeological interpretation.

In Périgord, François Vatar de Jouanet began to explore Pech de l'Azé as early as 1815 and set out the principle of a classification of knapped stone artefacts according to their types. In the Somme Valley around 1855, Jacques Boucher de Crèvecœur de Perthes (1788–1868) recorded the association,

within the same stratigraphic◆ level, of large Quaternary◆ animals (mammoth, rhinoceros, etc.) and flints worked by human beings, although that was not enough evidence to establish their absolute contemporaneousness. Along the same lines, Vicomte Alexis de Gourgue (1801–1885) sought to link archaeological and geological observations made in the vicinity of his château at Lanquais, in the Dordogne. It was, however, only in 1864 that Édouard Lartet's work on the site of La Madeleine provided more convincing arguments: the silhouette of a mammoth engraved on ivory proved that human beings had indeed lived alongside that animal.

Between 1869 and 1872 Gabriel de Mortillet (1821–1898) compiled stratigraphic, palaeontological, and typological data to propose the first archaeological classification of the Palaeolithic◆ era.

◆**Quaternary:**
The most recent geological era, lasting about 2 million years, characterised by alternating cold phases ("glaciations") and temperate phases ("interglacials") allowing mankind possibilities for development and territorial expansion. It is divided into two epochs, the Pleistocene (from the origins to 10,000 years ago) and the Holocene (from 10,000 years ago to the present).

La Vallée de la Vézère aux Eyzies, painting by J. Lapoque, 1860 (Périgueux, Musée du Périgord).

♦Palaeolithic: *Literally "the old stone age", the period prior to c. 10,000 years ago, characterised by the earliest known stone tool manufacture.*

The Vézère Valley, general map of the Palaeolithic sites, *Le Périgord préhistorique* by Otto Hauser, 1911.

At Les Eyzies, as elsewhere, prehistorians set out in search of the long sequences♦ necessary for providing a framework for prehistoric periods. Under the direction first of leading citizens, then of professionals, excavations followed one another fairly frenetically in the region until World War I. The huge quantities of frequently repetitive artefacts found gave rise to widespread movements of collections, sometimes sold, exchanged, or exported out of France, with no great benefit to science. The idea of preserving heritage or cultural property on the spot soon began to appear with the project for a first regional museum of prehistory at Les Eyzies, drawn up by Denis Peyrony. Peyrony, both a scholar and an efficient curator, was also concerned with making his work known to the general public and with setting the "world capital of prehistory" on the path of cultural tourism. He even organised public access to the most famous decorated caves and had electric lighting installed in Font-de-Gaume in 1920.

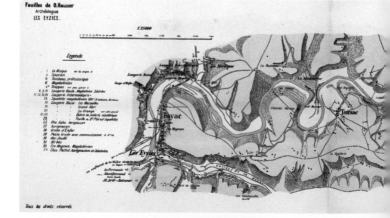

In the field Peyrony, an untiring excavator, later assisted by his son Élie, explored and elucidated the sequences of La Micoque, Laugerie-Haute, La Madeleine, Le Moustier, La Ferrassie, and other sites. In 1930 Raymond Vaufrey (1890–1967), professor of Quaternary geology and palaeontology at the Institut de paléontologie humaine, Paris, investigated a shelter with a well-developed stratigraphy at Cénac-et-Saint-Julien in the Dordogne Valley; it has since borne his name. The excavation of this cave porch was carried out between 1969 and 1981 by Jean-Philippe Rigaud, who continued work from 1992 to 2002 in Cave XVI in the same rocky massif. In addition to Maurice Bourgon's research, investigations directed by François Bordes from 1936 at Gavaudun, then at Combe-Capelle and, above all, between 1953 and 1965 at Combe-Grenal, Domme, Dordogne, must be mentioned. The Bordeaux University prehistory laboratory, where he taught, is indebted to him for its international prestige.

Concurrently with the efforts of multidisciplinary teams examining stratified sequences in rockshelter sites, some prehistorians turned, just after World War II, towards open-air sites and perceived the interest of studying them from a palaeoethnographic♦ point of view. From 1964—before Professor André Leroi-Gourhan's investigations at Pincevent, Seine-et-Marne—Dr Jean Gaussen excavated numerous Magdalenian camps in the Isle Valley, Dordogne, then published his findings.

Nowadays, increasingly varied disciplines are called upon: sedimentology (the study of the composition, structure, and texture of sediments), anthropology (the study of human remains), archaeozoology (the study of animal remains), typology (the classification of objects organised into types on the basis

Except where otherwise indicated, the documents and objects presented belong to the collections of the Musée national de Préhistoire.

| 5

Otto Hauser photographed during his excavations at La Micoque, 1906.

♦**Sequence:**
A series of archaeological and geological layers.

♦**Palaeoethnography:**
The reconstruction of ancient ways of life.

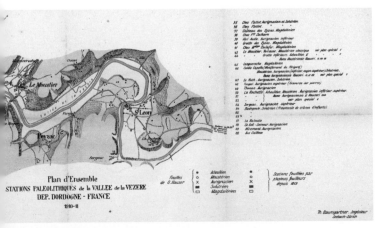

Plan d'Ensemble
STATIONS PALEOLITHIQUES de la VALLEE de la VEZERE
DEP. DORDOGNE - FRANCE
1910-11

♦Chaîne opératoire:
A form of lithic analysis that considers all stages of use from the initial collection of the raw material to the discarding of the unwanted tool.

♦Experimental archaeology:
The study of past behaviour through the reproduction and use of ancient tools, etc. under carefully controlled conditions.

of shared attributes), microwear analysis (the study of marks left on objects by their use), palynology (the analysis of fossil pollens and spores), etc. In France, teams from the various national scientific organisations study extremely varied subjects: the excavation of new sites, reassessment of old stratigraphic sections, detailed reconsideration of chronologies, studying the limits of and transitions between periods, seeking out the sources of raw materials, the economics of different cultures, the *chaîne opératoire*♦ of flint tool manufacture and, since 1990, experimental archaeology♦. A further step was taken thanks to archaeological excavations on Palaeolithic sites prior to work on the route of the future A89 motorway in the Dordogne Valley and of the Bergerac bypass, Dordogne.

Édouard Lartet (1801–1871)

Bust of Lartet, nineteenth-century sculpture (Saint-Germain-en-Laye, Musée des Antiquités nationales).

Le Moustier, print from *La Création de l'homme* by Henri du Cleuziou, 1887.

While at university, where he studied law (he practised as a lawyer until 1834), Édouard Lartet enthusiastically frequented scientific and naturalist circles in Toulouse and Paris. The early nineteenth century provided a particularly favourable context for debate. In 1809 Jean-Baptiste Lamarck (1744–1829) developed and applied to mankind the theory of evolution, according to which species descend from one another due to environmental causes. In this he was opposed to Georges Cuvier (1769–1832), in favour of the theory that mankind appeared later than the large vanished animals.

After years of collecting the bones of large mammals at Sansan, Gers, Édouard Lartet found a mandible belonging to Pliopithecus♦ confirming the existence of a Quadrumane♦ over 10 million years earlier.

He also participated in the founding of the science of prehistory with his work at Massat, Ariège, and Aurignac, Haute-Garonne, in 1860. That same year the paper he presented to the French academy of science on the great geological age of the human species in Western Europe received a mixed response from his colleagues.

In 1863 his acquaintance with Alexis de Gourgue (1801–1885), a native of Périgord, took him and his friend Henry Christy, a rich English industrialist, to the Vézère Valley.

A year later he proved the existence of a fossil man, contemporary with the great vanished animals, thanks to the discovery on the site of La Madeleine at Tursac, a few kilometres upstream from Les Eyzies, of a piece of ivory bearing the engraved image of a mammoth. He founded, as it were, the discipline of human palaeontology♦, but did not enjoy his fame for long. Lartet was already in poor health when he was appointed professor of palaeontology at the Muséum d'histoire naturelle, Paris, in 1868. He died in 1871 without having completed his major work, *Reliquiae Aquitanicae*, published in 1875 with the help of his son, Louis. The latter studied the burials in the Cro-Magnon rockshelter at Les Eyzies.

Large black cow with engraved outline, superimposed on horses, Lascaux, nave.

The discovery of Palaeolithic art

The first mobiliary♦ art was found in Périgord on the site of La Madeleine by Édouard Lartet and Henry Christy during the winter of 1863–4, in archaeological layers that had sometimes hardened into concretions or limestone formations, associated with vestiges of prehistoric industries. The first parietal♦ images in the cave of La Mouthe, at Les Eyzies, were brought to light by Émile Rivière in 1895, shortly after those at Altamira, Spain (1879), and Pair-non-Pair at Prignac-et-Marcamps, Gironde (1883), which were the subject of heated discussions. The cave of La Mouthe was visited by distinguished prehistorians such as Louis Capitan. The explorer of Laugerie-Basse, Élie Massenat, considered the images to be "rough sketches, caricatures of modern animals … which cannot be compared with the Magdalenian works of art". It was not until the discovery of the sanctuaries at Les Combarelles and Font-de-Gaume (8 and 12 September 1901) by Louis Capitan, the young Abbé Henri Breuil and Denis Peyrony that the existence of a parietal art form was established. The dispute lasted until the conference of the Association française pour l'avancement des sciences held in Périgueux in 1902. This recognition of parietal art opened the way for numerous discoveries: the caves of Bernifal (1902), Teyjat (1903), La Grèze (1904), and La Croze-à-Gontran (1908), and the rockshelters of Abri du Cap-Blanc (1910) and Abri du Poisson (1912). After Abbé Henri Breuil, the first specialist of Palaeolithic art, Professor André Leroi-Gourhan proposed, from 1958, a new approach to parietal symbolism, now overtaken by new theories. In France, nearly 200 decorated caves have been recorded so far—and discoveries are regularly announced (Cosquer, Chauvet, Cussac).

Mammoth, Les Combarelles, drawing by Abbé Breuil.

♦**Pliopithecus:** A variety of fossil monkey known at the end of the Tertiary era.

♦**Quadrumane:** A four-handed primate, i.e. with all four limbs ending in hands (ape).

♦**Palaeontology:** The study of the origins and evolution of extinct and fossil animals.

♦**Mobiliary and parietal art:** For archaeologists, prehistoric art is divided into these two main categories; the former consists of small portable objects, while the latter is found on the walls or ceilings of caves and shelters (or huge blocks of stone).

Excavation of Cave XVI at Cénac-et-Saint-Julien, in the Céou Valley.

Refitting♦ a Solutrean laurel leaf found during excavations on the Bergerac bypass route.

Pieces of worked flint during refitting, from excavations on the Bergerac bypass route.

Refitting (or conjoining): Attempting to put stone tools and flakes back together, providing information on tool manufacturing processes and relations between sectors of a site.

Palaeolithic cultures

Homo erectus
Early Palaeolithic—Acheulean
(600,000–250,000 years ago)

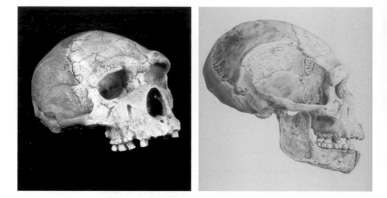

The reconstituted skull of the man discovered in 1971 in Caune de l'Arago, Tautavel (Centre européen de recherches préhistoriques de Tautavel).

♦Biface:
A stone tool, worked on two sides. It is characteristic of the Lower Palaeolithic, but was also used during the Middle Palaeolithic. It is also often called **handaxe** *in English.*

♦Flake: *A fragment of raw material removed from a larger stone or block (called* **core**, *see p. 12), often serving as blanks from which more complex tools could be made.*

♦Pebble tool:
A tool made by striking flakes from the edge of a pebble.

The earliest traces in Europe of our African ancestor, *Homo erectus*, have been recorded in Georgia (fossils from Dmanisi—between 1.8 million and 1.7 million years old) and in Spain (Orce—from about 1.2 million years ago). Other discoveries dating back 650,000 years have been reported at Atapuerca in Spain and Ceprano, to the north of Rome, Italy. It was however about 500,000 years ago that true occupation began. In France the largest number of human bones have been found in Caune de l'Arago, Tautavel, Pyrénées-Orientales: several dozen fragments of skeletons, including several skulls (with a capacity of about 1,150 cubic centimeters) are about 450,000 years old, associated with numerous stone tools. The lower levels (layers XI and XII) in Grotte Vaufrey, in the Dordogne, generally contemporary with Tautavel, held an industry consisting of bifaces♦, flakes♦, and pebble tools♦. Other archaeological sites dating from 350,000–300,000 years ago are known in Périgord: La Micoque, Combe-Grenal (lower levels), Vaufrey, Pech de l'Azé II, and Les Tares.

From that early date tools fall into two broad categories. On the one hand, tools could be shaped directly from the raw material (block or stone) by a series of blows made with a hammer, which could be hard (a river pebble) or soft (antler or wood),

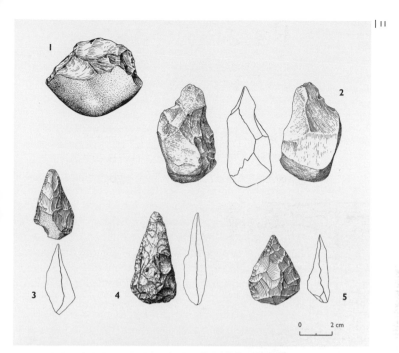

1. **Basalt chopper,** Pech de l'Azé II, layer 7.
2. **Middle Acheulean biface,** Pech de l'Azé II, layer 9.
3. **Micoquian biface,** La Micoque.
4. **Lanceolate Micoquian biface,** La Micoque.
5. **Cordiform ("heart-shaped") Micoquian biface,** La Micoque.

Acheulean biface, flint, 21 cm, Saint-Même-les-Carrières, Charente.

0   2 cm

⁺Cleaver:
A large bifacial tool with a transverse cutting edge.

⁺Core:
A block of hard stone, generally flint, from which flakes or blades have been removed after a certain amount of preparation. It may also be shaped to serve as an implement in its own right.

⁺Sidescraper:
A stone tool made from a flake retouched on one of its long sides.

⁺Eponym:
A person or place after whom or which a discovery, invention, place, etc. is named, originating in the Greek term epōnumos, meaning "which gives its name to something".

resulting in symmetrical objects, worked on two faces, with easily maintained cutting edges: typical Acheulean "bifaces". On the other, knapping produced variously shaped flakes that were either used in their initial state or retouched on the edges. The Micoquian and southern Acheulean forms developed alongside the "classical" Acheulean.

The concept of the southern province, defined by François Bordes some decades ago, continues to fuel debate. It is characterised by a few cleavers⁺ and above all by bifacial pieces, often with a triangular section. These are, firstly, the cores⁺ that provide flakes, later transformed into tools by bifacial retouches on one end. The Micoquian industry is defined by its very specific bifaces: intermediate models shaped with a soft hammer and often forming a sidescraper⁺—they are then called "backed" or "nucleiform" bifaces—are found alongside more classical types. On the eponym⁺ site, this industry seemed to be recent, dating at most to the start of the last glaciation, i.e. about 100,000 years ago, whereas in Central Europe very similar industries were considered to be 200,000 years older.

There is no evidence of the use of fire. Numerous traces of impact and scratching on bones prove that animals were consumed, whether deliberately hunted or scavenged as carrion.

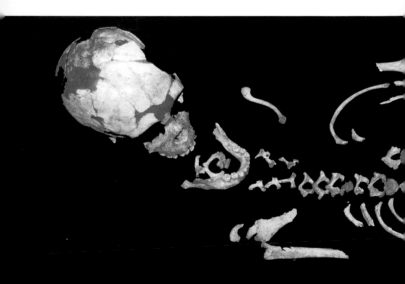

The Neanderthalers, *Homo sapiens neanderthalensis* Middle Palaeolithic—Mousterian (250,000–40,000 years ago)

Nowadays the transition from the Lower to the Middle Palaeolithic seems an increasingly theoretical question. The culture that is synonymous with the latter, the Mousterian, is called after two shelters near the village of Le Moustier, at the confluence of the Vézère and Vimont rivers. New dating methods have allowed the Mousterian chronology to be revised: in Périgord the oldest sites, earlier than the last interglacial, date back more than 200,000 years (Grotte Vaufrey, layers IX to II, and Les Tares). The Mousterian is also found at a more recent period: Cave XVI at Cénac-et-Saint-Julien, Combe-Grenal, and Pech de l'Azé. This culture is marked by a significant increase in the number of sites and the gradual occupation of all the ecological systems, which can be explained by technical progress—the domestication of fire, diversification of tools— and by the improved organisation of groups. The Mousterian corresponds to the maximum development of flake-based industries. The stone tools are made using several knapping methods with various retouches, to create most of the types known for the Palaeolithic. Improved management

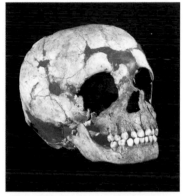

Skull and skeleton of the Neanderthal child from Roc de Marsal, Campagne, Dordogne.

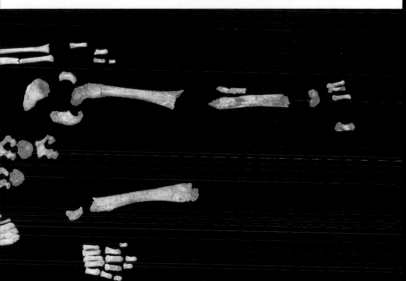

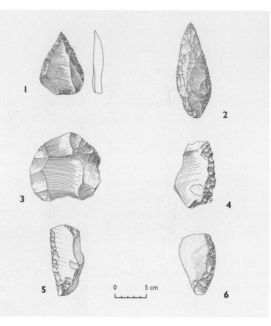

1. **Mousterian point,** Combe-Grenal, Typical Mousterian.
2. **Elongated Mousterian point,** Combe-Capelle, Mousterian of Acheulean tradition.
3. **Levallois core,** Combe-Grenal, La Ferrassie type Mousterian.
4. **Denticulate,** Pech de l'Azé, layer A, Mousterian of Acheulean tradition.
5. **Single straight sidescraper,** La Micoque, layer 4.
6. **Single convex sidescraper,** La Quina type, La Micoque, layers 4, 5.

♦Facies: *A term first developed for geological applications, used in archaeology to signify a subdivision of a culture or industry defined by diverse characteristics (tool assemblages, technology, etc.).*

of lithic raw materials led to the frequent "recycling" of tools: conversion from one type to another, modification and preparation in view of producing other supports. The rich variety and complexity of the Middle Palaeolithic was a result of this flexibility. This phenomenon reached its peak 80,000–40,000 years ago. In Aquitaine the exceptional diversity of facies♦ may reflect technological

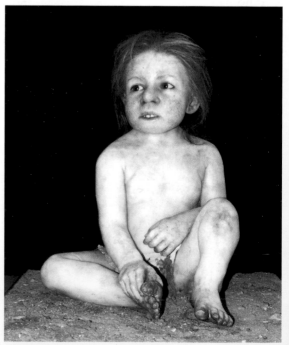

Reconstruction of the Neanderthal child from Roc de Marsal, Campagne, Dordogne.

Levallois core, flint from the Bergerac region, 12.5 cm.

choices made by the Mousterians. From about 100,000 years ago in the Near East, and more recently in Eastern then Western Europe, the first burials help improve our knowledge concerning the more recent Neanderthal populations.

Some 50,000 years ago Neanderthalers still occupied a territory spreading from the south of Spain to Kurdistan and from northern Europe to Palestine. Of sturdy stature, with a brain size superior or equal to our own, Neanderthalers presented many morphological differences with modern humans, but none that denote any physical or intellectual inferiority. Neanderthalers were the first people in Europe to bury their dead and to use colouring materials. They lived in socially structured groups and seem to have taken care of their old and sick.

Woolly rhinoceros from Starunia, Poland, replica.

In France, Neanderthalers occupied the whole of the mainland and began to enter the underground world. Groups travelled over a moderately large territory, less than 100 kilometres in radius, and frequented in turn dwellings—rarely featuring specific installations although controlled fire was present—and scavenging and hunting sites, specialised or otherwise, often close to sources of raw materials. Supplies of flint, mainly local, varied depending on the resources available and the activities pursued. When the raw material came from a distance exceeding ten kilometres it was transported in the form of worked artefacts (retouched tools, bifaces, flakes, often of the Levallois* type, etc.). Apart from hard stone, Neanderthalers also used wood (handles,

*****Levallois flake:** A flake of predetermined shape and size, obtained from a specially prepared core.

Châtelperron points, Grotte des Fées, Châtelperron, Allier, after H. Delporte and photographs.

♦**Interstadial:** *An intermediate milder phase during a cold period.*

♦**Radiocarbon dating:** *A dating method based on the measurement of the residual radioactivity of the carbon isotope 14 (C14) contained in organic materials. Because the radioactivity of C14 diminishes over time, the method cannot be applied to objects more than 40,000 years old.*

♦**Relative or absolute chronology:** *Absolute dates allow time to be determined quantitatively (i.e. in years), although with a certain lack of precision, by methods based on physics and physico-chemistry (radiocarbon, thermoluminescence, etc.) or other data (dendrochronology, or tree-ring dating, the study of annual growth rings in trees). Relative dates measure differences in age, for example by using stratigraphy.*

♦**Châtelperron point:** *An abrupt retouched backed blade forming a point.*

hafts, shafts for spears, etc.) and perishable materials (adhesive, bitumen, or pitch, for hafting tools). They were sometimes fishermen but above all hunters of large herbivores, which supplied meat, skins, furs, and bones. The bones, after extraction of the marrow, were sometimes used as hammers and, more rarely, to make tools. The first stirrings of symbolic observances are perceptible in the funerary domain, in the form of portable objects (offerings?) placed deliberately in graves. In addition, objects are also found for which any utilitarian function is debatable (colouring materials, natural curiosities such as fossils, quartz crystals, etc.), although their underlying significance, in particular in burials, remains a mystery.

The last Neanderthalers Middle to Upper Palaeolithic transition—Châtelperronian (around 40,000 years ago)

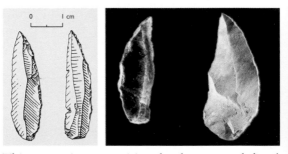

This mysterious transitional culture was defined from the Grotte des Fées site at Châtelperron, Allier. The Châtelperronian presents a laminar industry with a knapping technique that seems similar to that of the Middle Palaeolithic. It suffers from two handicaps: it appeared at the end of the last interstadial♦, during a temperate and humid period (the archaeological deposits are thus practically non-existent), and falls on the borderline of the field of application of radiocarbon dating methods♦. No relative or absolute chronology♦ thus exists for this period. Mainly identified in Aquitaine, northern Spain, and Italy, it could be the consequence of Mousterians adopting a technical innovation, the Châtelperron point♦, which could serve as a knife or projectile tip. On a European scale, it could be envisaged, on the basis of imprecise absolute dates, that the last Neanderthalers were contemporary with the first *sapiens sapiens*. There is no evidence of either violent relations or intermarriage between

these two human groups. In Aquitaine, the latest stratigraphic reappraisals invalidate the theory of the contemporaneousness of the Châtelperronian and Aurignacian industries, and thus call into question the possible coexistence of their makers.

The confluence of the Vézère and Beune rivers during a glacial period (above) and during an interglacial (below), watercolours by A. Dalis.

Cro-Magnon man, *Homo sapiens sapiens* Upper Palaeolithic

Upper Palaeolithic—Aurignacian (35,000–28,000 years ago)

During this period Europe was the scene for deep-seated cultural and biological upheavals marked by the arrival of *Homo sapiens sapiens*. Following the last cultures attributed to the Neanderthalers,

Reconstituted skeleton of a steppe bison, La Berbie, Castel, Dordogne.

the Aurignacian culture brings together all the criteria of modernity with the expression of an externalised symbolic way of thinking—personal ornaments and various forms of artistic expression (painting, sculpture in the round, engraving on all types of supports, mainly with figurative depictions of animals, signs, and some human figures)—new technologies—laminar and lamellar lithic industry, the generalisation of a bone industry—and complex social rules. Relative knowledge regarding dwellings in caves or in the open (organised around the practically systematic presence of a hearth), extremely diversified subsistence activities, and reindeer hunting (dominant in Aquitaine), should not conceal the true facts. In Western Europe, no burial can be attributed to the Aurignacian culture and no fossil *sapiens sapiens* has yet been associated with it. Does this culture correspond to a migrant population that occupied the whole of Europe or, on the contrary, to a set of values shared by different groups of human beings? Whatever the case, Aurignacian societies inaugurated a period providing numerous elements defining the Upper Palaeolithic as a whole.

Endscraper on a strangulated blade, 12.3 cm (left), La Ferrassie, and **Aurignacian bone tools,** 16.2 cm for the largest.

Upper Palaeolithic—Gravettian
(28,000–23,000 years ago)

This culture is found from the Iberian Peninsula to the Altai Mountains, Iran, and the Near East, with numerous regional entities over this huge territory. In south-western France, the Gravettian stage is also called "Perigordian". The lithic industry is characterised by blade-like supports, some of which, straight and flat, allowed the making

Microgravettes and Gravette points, 2.9 cm for the largest, Laugerie-Haute East, Les Eyzies, Dordogne.

"The Laussel Venus" (female figure holding a bison horn), Laussel, Dordogne (Bordeaux, Musée d'Aquitaine).

of straight-backed points, called "Gravette points" (projectile tips, backed with abrupt retouches defining a point). The bone industry in Western Europe is less abundant and varied than that in Central or Eastern Europe; it consists of awls and long spears, sometimes with an oblique base. Mobiliary art is represented by decoration on utilitarian objects (spears, *bâtons percés*•, etc.) but above all by female statuettes, called "Venus figurines", made from various stones, ivory, or antler. Parietal art, engraved, carved and/or painted, presents the classical animal themes and many positive and negative hand prints•. It is not restricted to shelters, but penetrates deep

♦Bâton percé (or bâton perforé):
An antler cylinder, often decorated, with a hole pierced through the thickest part; its function is still a matter for discussion.

♦Hand prints:
Prints on cave walls are based on the "stencil" principle, and may be positive or negative. For the former, the hand was coated with pigment then applied to the surface; for the latter, pigment was projected over the hand.

Font-Robert point, 8.4 cm, Le Flageolet, Bezenac, Dordogne.

into the underground world, as at Cussac, Gargas, and Pech-Merle. Movements of raw materials point to communications over distances exceeding 300 kilometres.

Upper Palaeolithic—Solutrean
(23,000–18,500 years ago)

The Solutrean was identified for the first time at Solutré, Saône-et-Loire, but in fact extended south-wards, covering the perimeter of the Iberian Peninsula

Aurochs carved in low relief, 1.3 m × 0.72 m, Fourneau du Diable, Bourdeilles, Dordogne.

⁺Laurel leaf:
A delicately retouched leaf-shaped point, used as a projectile tip or knife.

⁺Shouldered point:
An asymmetric point that narrows at its base to allow hafting.

⁺Willow leaf:
A leaf-shaped point for a projectile.

Laurel leaf,
7.6 cm, Fourneau du Diable, Bourdeilles, Dordogne.

and Italy's Ligurian coast, only reaching as far north as the south of the Paris Basin. Its origin and development are still subject to debate. The climate during this period was particularly unreliable, with cold dry periods alternating with humid ones. These climatic conditions may have led the Solutreans to prefer natural shelters over dwellings in the open.

Teyjat,
Late Magdalenian landscape.

The Solutreans roamed over huge geographical areas to hunt large herbivores, but also to collect high-quality flint and rare products. No burials are definitely attributed to them, but Solutrean art, apart from decorated caves, testifies to special interest in engraving and monumental sculpture (Fourneau du Diable at Bourdeilles in the Dordogne, and the large Roc de Sers shelter in Charente). The Solutrean is characterised by flat points, known as "laurel leaves"*, microlithic projectile tips, and knives made by bifacial shaping complemented, depending on the item in question, by pressure retouches and heat treatment of the flint. Shouldered points* and "willow leaves"* points, typical of the Late Solutrean, attest to a new method of hafting. Inventions such as the eyed sewing needle and the spearthrower*, objects that came into more general use during the Magdalenian period, also date from this period.

Spearthrower: | 23
An implement with a hook, often made of bone and decorated, used to increase the power with which a projectile can be thrown.

Upper Palaeolithic—Magdalenian (18,500–11,000 years ago)

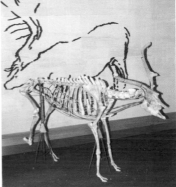

Reconstituted skeleton of a reindeer, Le Quéroy, Chazelles, Charente.

This is the most famous of the prehistoric cultures, and the best documented thanks to the discovery of several remarkable sites, both under rockshelters and in the open, as well as many decorated caves. Its name comes from the site of La Madeleine, upstream from Les Eyzies, on the banks of the Vézère. The geographical area covered by the Magdalenian

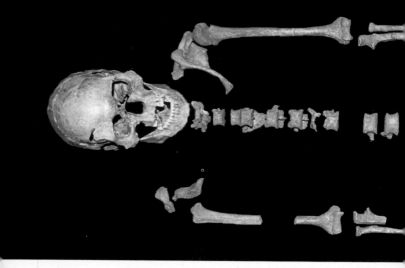

Skeleton of the Magdalenian adolescent from Roc de Cave, Saint-Cirq-de-Madelon, Lot. **Bison licking its side,** La Madeleine. **Flint tools** from the Upper Magdalenian, 7.2 cm for the largest, Laugerie-Basse.

♦**Blade, bladelet:** Elongated and fairly thin flakes, struck from a core.

♦**Burin:** A lithic tool with one end shaped by the removal of small chips of stone, called spalls, to form a sort of chisel.

♦**Endscraper:** An instrument made by retouches on the end of a flake or blade.

♦**Parrot-beak:** A burin with a spall removal running towards the interior of the implement.

♦**Tanged point:** A microlith with one end thinned for hafting.

and its regional density have little in common with the Solutrean. The Magdalenian is found throughout Western Europe. This culture, contemporary with the end of the last glaciation and the start of the warming-up of the atmosphere that followed, is broken down into several subdivisions on the basis of cultural criteria.

The lithic industry is based on blades♦ or bladelets♦. The early phase contains large numbers of burins♦ and endscrapers♦, associated with triangular microliths (miniaturised arms and flints of the Late Palaeolithic and Mesolithic periods, in the form of points, triangles, or trapezes). Dihedral burins (with two plane faces), with a bevel formed by the intersection of two spall removals, dominate in the Middle Magdalenian, then microlithic industries emerge in the Upper and Late Magdalenian (Laugerie-Basse points, parrot-beak burins♦, tanged Teyjat points♦).

Artefacts made from bone and reindeer antler increase in number and become more diversified, culminating in complex objects such as harpoons.

Mobiliary or parietal art included masterpieces of realism. Ornaments are frequently associated with human remains. They are generally seashells accompanied by pierced teeth, ivory beads, etc.

These hunter-gatherers roamed over huge territories in search of lithic materials and, especially, animals such as reindeer, saiga antelope, aurochs (the extinct wild ancestor of domestic cattle, *Bos primigenius*), horses, deer, and elk, not forgetting small game; they also fished on a large scale.

The great discoverers

Denis Peyrony (1869–1954), a scholarly teacher

Denis Peyrony.

Mere coincidence or a sign of destiny, the most famous prehistorian of Périgord was born in the village of Cussac, which became famous in 2001 when its sanctuary (containing engravings and burials) was discovered intact. While a young schoolmaster at Les Eyzies-de-Tayac he was "infected" by the distinguished prehistorians he regularly frequented, in particular Dr Louis Capitan (1854–1929). He discovered, alone or with others, several major sites, such as the caves of Les Combarelles and Font-de-Gaume. From the early twentieth century he participated in debates on the recognition of prehistoric parietal art and the establishment of a chronological framework and dates based on stratigraphy and material cultures.

At the same time as his scientific contributions in the field, he must be credited with bringing to a successful conclusion detailed publications. Thanks to his teaching talents, he wrote works aimed at all types of readers. Peyrony combined all the tasks that would today be divided between various regional or

Denis Peyrony's excavations at La Ferrassie in 1910.

Denis Peyrony in front of the stratigraphic section at Le Moustier.

national agencies responsible for archaeology, historic monuments, or museums. He pleaded for the protection of the archaeological heritage—caves, sites, and movable objects—quite rightly recommending the maintaining of the major Palaeolithic collections in their region of origin. In 1913 he initiated the regional prehistory museum at Les Eyzies, the future Musée national de Préhistoire, and also helped the state define its role in heritage conservation, whether in the domain of protection or in the encouragement of scientific research. His son Élie became curator of the museum and participated in further excavations.

Abbé Henri Breuil (1877–1961),
"the pope of prehistory"

Abbé Breuil, aged 20.

Henri Breuil took an interest in archaeology from a very early age and began research into the Bronze Age in the Somme Valley. In 1897 he set off on a tour of the famous archaeological sites of south-western France with some prehistorian friends. From then onwards, his life was mapped out: a religious vocation confirmed in 1900, a doctoral thesis on the prehistoric art of the "age of the reindeer" in 1904, work on the Somme terraces, the establishment of the subdivisions of the Palaeolithic era, and research into parietal art in France, Spain, South Africa, etc.

He was appointed to the chair of prehistory at the Collège de France in 1929, then became a member of the Institut de France. He continued his explorations in the Vézère Valley and authenticated many discoveries, including that of Lascaux. He published his theories on decorated caves in *Quatre Cents Siècles d'art pariétal* ("Four Hundred Centuries of Parietal Art") in 1952. "The pope of prehistory", as he was dubbed at the end of his life, died, aged 84, at L'Isle-Adam, leaving a monumental oeuvre behind him.

Abbé Henri Breuil and Comte Bégouën in the cave at Lascaux and at its exit with two of the discoverers, Jacques Marsal and Marcel Ravidat, accompanied by their schoolmaster, Léon Laval, on 28 October 1940.

François Bordes (1919–1981),
the prehistorian-geologist

François Bordes in 1977 (Jean-Philippe Rigaud Collection).

After having presented his doctoral thesis on the Quaternary alluvia of the Seine Basin at the end of World War II, François Bordes turned to the study of the typology of Early and Middle Palaeolithic industries. Appointed professor at the Bordeaux university of the sciences, he founded the Institut de préhistoire et de géologie du Quaternaire and became interested in the classification and definition of lithic industries. In 1961 he observed that very few of the types of tools long considered as absolutely characteristic of the various periods of the Palaeolithic could be relied on, but that what in fact did seem characteristic were the ratios between the various types of artefacts found. He then developed a method based on a list of lithic artefact types for the Early and Middle Palaeolithic, later extended by his wife, Denise de Sonneville-Bordes, to cover the Upper Palaeolithic. It is thus possible to use the frequency indices of the various artefacts and cumulative percentage diagrams that allow series to be compared. Bordes directed many excavations, including those in the rockshelter of Combe-Grenal, Domme, and the Pech de l'Azé cave at Carsac, in the Dordogne Valley to the south of Sarlat. Their long stratigraphical sections served to define in particular several facies of the Mousterian culture.

From André Glory to Jean Gaussen

A follower of Henri Breuil, **André Glory** (1906–1966) explored several caves in southwestern France and settled in the Dordogne. Between 1952 and 1963 he deciphered and recorded on tracing paper the entangled engravings in Lascaux, spending about 5,000 hours on this task. His accidental death prevented him from publishing his monograph on Lascaux and work on the cave of Roucadour, Lot. His archives have recently been found and are being studied. **Louis-René Nougier** (1912–1995), founder of the Institut d'art préhistorique, Toulouse, discovered the drawings and engravings in the huge cave of Rouffignac, Dordogne. **Claude Barrière** succeeded him as professor of prehistoric archaeology at Toulouse and published numerous works on parietal art.

Séverin Blanc (1893–1970), a former teacher at Les Eyzies and local politician in the Dordogne, challenged the authenticity of the drawings of mammoths in the cave of Rouffignac, disagreeing with Abbé Breuil.

André Leroi-Gourhan and Brigitte Delluc in the cave at Les Combarelles (Brigitte and Gilles Delluc Collection).

With Marcel Vidal, he discovered the Mesolithic skeleton of Roc du Barbeau, in the Combe de Vergne at Le Moustier.

Following work by **Annette Laming Emperaire**, Professor **André Leroi-Gourhan** (1911–1986) refused to assimilate parietal art with hunting magic, totemism, or shamanism and attempted to demonstrate that the depictions comply with a well-defined schema, including deliberate associations and compositions. In 1964 he published *Les Religions de la préhistoire* and *Le Geste et la Parole* (respectively "The Religions of Prehistory" and "Gesture and Speech"); in 1966 a monumental work appeared,

La Préhistoire de l'art occidental (published in English in 1968 as *The Art of Prehistoric Man in Western Europe*), the fruit of ten years' work. His chronology and interpretations have now been partially called into question after the discoveries of further important caves and reconsideration of dating methods.

Dr **Jean Gaussen** (1919 2000) is an iconic figure for archaeology in the Dordogne. He discovered and excavated, for the first time in France, surface dwelling sites dating to the Upper Palaeolithic in the Isle Valley and published an outstanding study of the decorated cave of Le Gabillou at Sourzac, near Mussidan, Dordogne.

André Leroi-Gourhan in the cave at Les Combarelles (Brigitte and Gilles Delluc Collection).

Engraved hemione (wild ass, also called kiang), Le Gabillou cave, Sourzac, Dordogne (Jean Gaussen Collection).

Les Combarelles, detail, drawing by Claude Barrière (C. Barrière Collection).

Jean Gaussen in Le Gabillou cave, Dordogne (Marie-Louise Gaussen Collection).

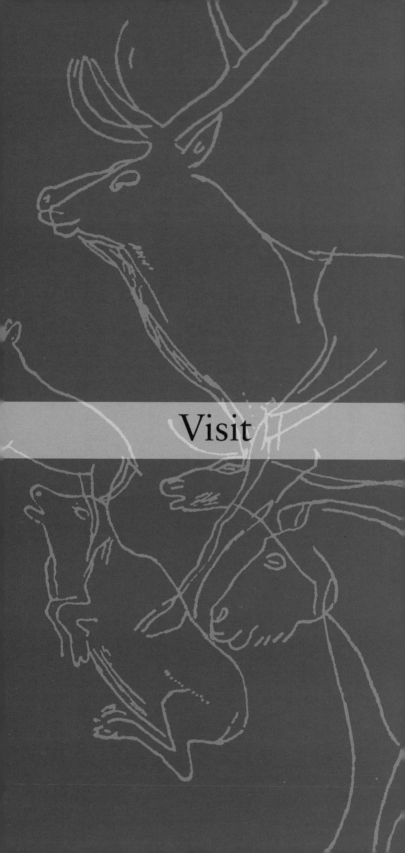

Visit

La Micoque, or the first inhabitants of Périgord

The year 1895 saw the discovery of this major site at Les Eyzies, following the uprooting of a vineyard. It was the first truly stratified, reliable, and coherent human settlement, found in a context that was quite unforeseen at the time, being neither a cave nor a rockshelter. Establishing a chronostratigraphic framework for the Early and Middle Palaeolithic periods was by then already a major challenge: this site, doubly eponymous—for the Tayacian[*] (attributed to the Early Palaeolithic) and the Micoquian (the hypothetical end of that period)—warranted various thorough excavation campaigns leading to the exhaustion of the Micoquian layer. With its highly specific bifaces shaped with a soft hammer and often forming a sidescraper, this seemed recent and was believed to date back at most to the start of the last glaciation, around 100,000 years ago; that gave credence to its transitional aspect between the Early and Middle Palaeolithic, whereas in Central Europe industries that are morphologically very similar were considered to be 200,000 years older. The explanation for this chronological distortion was

found when excavations were resumed between 1986 and 1995 by a team from the Institut de préhistoire et de géologie du Quaternaire de Bordeaux. The results, now being published, are exceptionally interesting as they update twentieth-century established scientific facts and define a reliable and coherent chronological framework based on some thirty absolute dates obtained by ESR[*].

The occupation levels correspond to the repeated installation of human beings on a rocky bar on the edge of the flood plain of a river (now the Manaurie): at the time it consisted of interlaced channels with contrasting seasonal flow patterns, typical of a cold, semi-arid climate.

[*]Tayacian:
A prehistoric cultural group defined on the site of La Micoque, near Tayac, characterised by a flake-based knapping technique.

[*]ESR (electron spin resonance dating):
A method depending on radioactive decay, based on the measurement of trapped electrons and allowing various materials (e.g. bone, teeth, shell, etc.) to be dated as far back as 400,000 years ago.

Typical Micoquian biface with lanceolate edges, 9.5 cm.

Stratigraphic schema of the site,
after Texier and Rigaud

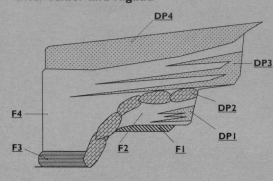

DP4

DP3

DP2

DP1

F4

F3

F2

F1

F1 F2 DP1

Layers I to XII
for Laville and Rigaud (1969).

F3 F4 DP3

Layers A to N
for Peyrony (1938).
Layer E:
c. 400,000 years ago,
southern Acheulean.
Layer H (crushed):
290,000–280,000
years ago, Tayacian
for Peyrony.
Layer N (crushed):
Micoquian.

♦*Discoid technique:*
A technique for knapping flakes of stone, in which the block of raw material is turned regularly, giving it a circular form.

♦*Clactonian:*
An industrial facies first described on the site of Clacton-on-Sea, Essex, England, characterised by the knapping of thick flakes of stone.

Dating from around 400,000 years ago, layer E (fairly close to layer D) presents a low degree of typological diversity: single or convex scaled retouched sidescrapers are preponderant, accompanied by numerous notches, often intensively used, and a few bifaces (in the earliest series). The Mousterian appearance was confirmed in recent excavations where, as in the other levels,

the characteristic southern Acheulean knapping technique is mixed with discoid♦ and Clactonian♦ techniques. Layer L, dated to 290,000–280,000 years ago, corresponding to Peyrony's Tayacian, also presents knapping characteristic of the southern Acheulean and the shaping of bifacial artefacts, including backed tools; the generally crushed aspect can be attributed to strong disturbance due to fluviatile activity.

♦*Oxygen isotope chronology:*
Certain marine fossils (Foraminifera) have recorded variations in the temperature of surface waters in their shells (oxygen isotopes 16 and 18). Measurements of these variations in deep-sea cores of marine sediments, chronologically positioned by palaeomagnetism (the record of variations in the earth's magnetic polarity), have allowed 37 major variations (isotopic stages) to be defined, covering 1.67 million years.

Jean-Pierre Texier's geological study of the fill revealed three interlocked accumulations of sediments with overlapping fluviatile silt and colluvial deposits from slopes in the form of lateral passages that are sometimes tricky to interpret. The lower and median groups, containing practically no fossils, are separated by a clayey formation corresponding to a hollowed-out section partially filled in with large blocks, synonymous with a temperate episode separating two cold semi-arid phases. In the oxygen isotope chronology♦, these three levels can be attributed respectively to stages XII (470,000–400,000 years ago), XI (440,000–370,000 years ago), and X (370,000–350,000 years ago). Only the median accumulation contains evidence of human activity and presents three archaeological layers

already identified by Peyrony under the names E, H, and L. The upper accumulation, which contained the renowned Micoquian industries, has been exhausted, but remnants of the same sedimentary formation, containing no fossils, have survived on the periphery of the site. Investigations have revealed absolutely no traces of deep-seated freezing. They are therefore probably recent colluvial deposits, and in no way date from the Pleistocene. The Micoquian layer (Peyrony's layer N) probably only consisted of disturbed sediments from the overlying slopes, now in a secondary position. The myth of a transitional industry between the Early and Middle Palaeolithic periods has had its day. Our improved perception of the ways of life of the craftsmen responsible for that industry,

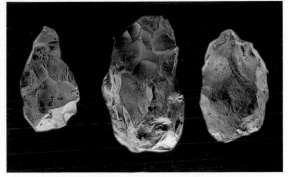

thanks to the study of bone remains discovered on the site, represents further progress due to the recent excavations. Horses seem clearly to have dominated, always associated with other ungulates (aurochs, bovids, deer, reindeer, and an extinct species of Equidae similar to the donkey), to which may be added a rhinoceros and a member of the Elephantidae. There is no evidence of the use of fire at La Micoque, but the many marks of impacts and scratching on the bones attest to the consumption of marrow.

Bifaces
from La Micoque, 13.2 cm for the largest.

Refitting of flakes
on their core, Grotte Vaufrey.

The two shelters at Le Moustier

A few kilometres away from Les Eyzies these two shelters, one of which is called "classical" and the other "lower", have usurped the name of a small village at the confluence of the Vézère and Vimont rivers, although in fact they are attached administratively to the neighbouring municipality of Saint-Léon-sur-Vézère. This lasting misapprehension is perhaps due to the prehistorian Gabriel de Mortillet (1821–1898).

Speaking in Paris in 1868–9 of the classical dwelling, now exhausted archaeologically, he endorsed it as the eponym site for Neanderthal cultures. At the foot of the cliff, in the lower shelter, Otto Hauser began work in 1907 with his usual hasty methods. A year later the remains of a Neanderthaler appeared. The Swiss antiquary organised a presentation: scientific experts and potential clients, all Germanic, were invited to the final disinterment.

Le Moustier, the classical shelter

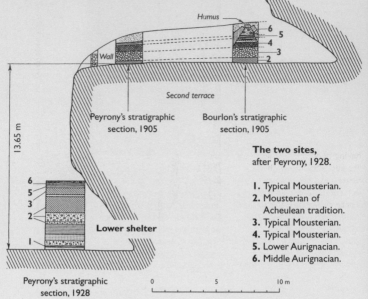

Humus

Wall

Second terrace

Peyrony's stratigraphic section, 1905

Bourlon's stratigraphic section, 1905

13.65 m

Lower shelter

Peyrony's stratigraphic section, 1928

0   5   10 m

The two sites,
after Peyrony, 1928.

1. Typical Mousterian.
2. Mousterian of Acheulean tradition.
3. Typical Mousterian.
4. Typical Mousterian.
5. Lower Aurignacian.
6. Middle Aurignacian.

According to the sedimentologist Henri Laville, the sequence was organised in two series of deposits that could be dated to the early part of the Würm Glaciation. The lower sequence (layers A to F, consisting of fluviatile alluvial sediments, sometimes stratified with a little scree), groups several archaeological layers (Typical and Denticulate Mousterian) attributable to Würm I; layer G (containing Mousterian of Acheulean tradition, Type A) belongs chronologically to the same layers, but is already part of the upper sedimentary deposit. The upper and most legible sequence (layers G to K), essentially cryoclastic in origin (i.e. formed of broken limestone fragments detached from the walls by successive freezing and thawing over the ages), apparently the coldest, is attributable to Würm II and contains the same lithic industries as the earlier ones, supplemented by Mousterian of Acheulean tradition, Type B. Topping the whole, two fairly disturbed archaeological layers contained a heterogeneous mixture of Châtelperronian and Mousterian (layer K) and typical Aurignacian from layer L. This was thus thought to be a reliable and coherent framework probably covering a chronology of over 50,000 years, from the beginning of the last glaciation to the arrival of *Homo sapiens sapiens* around 34,000 BC.

"A Mousterians' congress"

♦Assemblage: A group of artefacts that can be considered a single unit for analysis.

The site of Combe-Grenal, near Domme, contains a sequence covering the period 110,000–45,000 years ago. More than fifty strata yielded a wide diversity of industrial assemblages♦, to the point that François Bordes described it as "a Mousterians' congress". This diversity was interpreted as corresponding to different types of human behaviour and human mobility over hunting grounds: the existence of robust tools demanding a large amount of raw material in certain levels suggested rather static occupations, while others seemed to point to more itinerant activities; sidescrapers and points, for example, were perceived as hunting implements.

The success was such that the operation was repeated several times, each with an official report, on 7 March, 6 June, 3 July, and 10 August 1908, after "a hearty meal with plenty of wine".

It is thus easier to understand why "the pelvis and spine crumbled into dust".

A pity for this Neanderthaler who, during his second life, suffered from the bombing raids of 1945 without ever having been comprehensively studied, although he had provoked two debates, in quite different registers. These related, on the one hand, to the intentionality of the burial, laying the foundations for the concept of a less brutish or ape-like human, and, on the other, to the conservation of heritage remains *in situ*, with more nationalistic scientists being opposed to partisans of "science without frontiers", the latter in effect approving the fossil's export to Germany. The French government purchased the site in 1910 and Peyrony was then able to proceed with more serious excavations. He did not accord much importance to the discovery of a limestone slab coloured with manganese oxide, perhaps the first evidence of symbolic expression by Neanderthalers, or to a truly exceptional Neanderthal perinatal skeleton found in the reserves of the Musée national de Préhistoire after more than a century of oblivion.

In fact, the importance of this perfectly stratified eponym site lay elsewhere: seven metres of stratigraphy founded in effect the chronostratigraphic basis and the constitutive principle of "the Mousterian". In his typological classification François Bordes, following in the footsteps of Maurice Bourgon, had from 1950 underlined the apparent coexistence of diversified industries, expressions of technical activities, but also capable of bearing chronological implications, for the presence

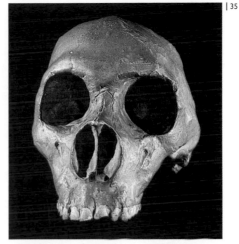

Skull of a Neanderthal man from Le Moustier.

at Le Moustier of several "types" of interstratified Mousterian opened the door to hypotheses supported by the stratigraphic revision of 1969. In 1992, however, their interpretation was modified by the absolute dating by thermoluminescence[♦] of some thirty burnt flints. The upper sequence was probably set in place no later than 15,000–20,000 years ago, layers K and H 40,000–46,000 years ago, while the Mousterian of Acheulian tradition of level G dates back at most to 56,000 years ago. It is now clear that there is no correlation between age and Mousterian facies: the Mousterian variants are probably the indication of diversified technical activities within a more or less homogeneous mode of subsistence. These differences may well reflect seasonal behaviour.

While the debate is now open, the "revised" stratigraphy of this eponym site has put an end to long-standing discussions that had encumbered archaeological research for decades. The remaining few square metres of archaeological stratigraphy were well worth the detour.

♦**Thermoluminescence:**
A dating technique relying indirectly on radioactive decay, based on the fact that, when stimulated, electrons trapped in the structure of certain minerals that have previously been subjected to heating can be released in the form of light. By measuring the amount of this light and the quantity of radioactive material present, it is possible to establish the time that has elapsed since the material was last heated.

Stratigraphic section of the site, Savignac-de-Miremont, Le Bugne, Dordogne.

La Ferrassie: the Neanderthal culture and the first expressions of spirituality

This imposing if rather isolated site, some fifteen kilometres from Les Eyzies, does not figure on the UNESCO inventory, although everything—from its history and remarkable stratigraphy to the exceptional finds made there, which shed new light on the spiritual life of prehistoric populations—destined it for such an honour. The site acquired its reputation with Denis Peyrony's work between 1896 and 1921.

The general outline of the sequence was established in 1912: it falls approximately between those of Le Moustier and Laugerie-Haute (see pages 33 and 44). The survey published by Peyrony in 1934 is founded on observations in the field: strata individualised among the fourteen layers include two Mousterian levels (including the scraper-dominated "Ferrassie" Charentian), several levels for the Aurignacian (from the early phases to Aurignacian IV) and Upper Perigordian or Gravettian, establishing the evolution of this culture

on the basis of the presence of index fossils♦, Font-Robert points, truncated elements, and Noailles burins.

Between 1968 and 1973 Henri Delporte, in a painstaking attempt to refine Peyrony's sequence further, resumed excavations under difficult conditions. He came up against the complexity of the fill, presenting numerous lateral variations; the correlation between the levels in different sectors verges on the contradictory. Sedimentological studies undertaken during this work deciphered ten sedimentary phases, corresponding to diverse climatic fluctuations (cold, humid, and dry). Published in 1998, the lithostratigraphic review♦ of the site by Jean-Pierre Texier became more realistic by simplifying things. Only three sedimentary units are defined: top, median, and lower. The classical chronoclimatic♦ interpretation thus seems to require general reconsideration: the composition of the fill

♦**Index fossil:**
A notion used in biostratigraphic classifications and extended to archaeological artefacts considered typical of a given culture or period.

♦**Lithostratigraphic review:**
Review of the formation of deposits of different stones in the filling of a stratigraphic section.

♦**Chronoclimatic:**
Referring to a sequence of types of climates over time.

and its evolution suggest a sedimentary cone[*], moving as the line of the shelter roof receded, whence the easily visible flow marks along the rocks and the brecciation of certain strata.

The archaeological implications are thus obvious: the homogeneity of the archaeological levels must be considered with caution, for there is an obvious risk of the redistribution of material by dynamic processes, notably the splitting of levels; moreover, the correlation between the two stratigraphic sections remains tricky, all the more so since the rate of burial and sedimentation seems to be variable depending on the different zones of the site.

The upper sector was therefore probably set in place by rock falls and running water. The median unit seems to have been generated by the piling up of solifluction[*] gullies with stony fronts, including a caving-in episode and the destruction of the distal section[*] by seasonally running water (snow thawing, heavy rain).

The lower unit appears to be an accumulation of gravity-drawn blocks filled in by the percolation of fine particles, interstratified with organic beds from the archaeological levels (the latter are due to human activity, but cryoturbated[*] and subject to solifluction). The environmental evidence points to a generally cold atmosphere, with some short, more temperate fluctuations. The fundamental information provided by Peyrony's excavations in the artistic and anthropological domains is in no way called into question: to this day La Ferrassie remains the reference site for studying Neanderthal populations in Western Europe. Without being perfectly synchronous, the seven individuals discovered there provide an exceptionally full picture of a fossil population, including adults of both sexes and children from the foetal stage to early adolescence. The "old man" of La Ferrassie, aged about forty-five, suffered from a state of physical deterioration precluding independent survival:

[*]**Sedimentary cone:**
A geological deposit of materials in the form of a cone.

[*]**Solifluction:**
The gradual movement of wet soil etc. down a slope.

[*]**Distal section:**
The end, the most distant part.

[*]**Cryoturbated archaeological level:**
A level in which artefacts and other archaeological evidence have been displaced due to the effects of alternating phases of freezing and thawing.

Stratigraphic sections, after Peyrony, 1934

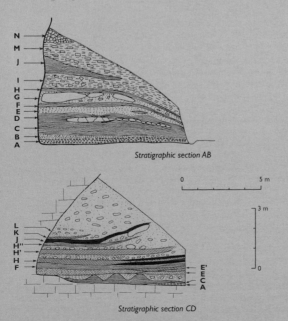

Stratigraphic section AB

Stratigraphic section CD

Layer A:
coarse scree, carbonated and sterile.
Group B, C:
fine limestone gravel, enriched with fine sediments, three metres thick, containing the Perigordian industry.
Group D, E:
marked variations.
Group F, G, H, J, K:
corresponding to the Aurignacian I to IV layers.
Group L, M:
containing the Châtelperronian and Mousterian industries.

38 | **Plan of the site** showing the disposition of the structures and the location of the burials.
1. Burials.
2. Edge of the roof.
3. Enclosure.
4. Pits.

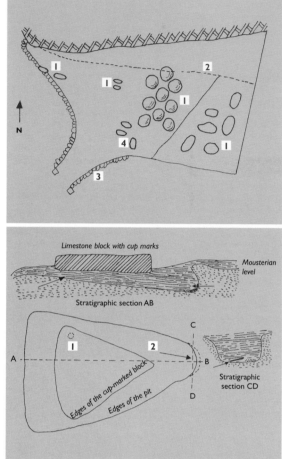

Limestone block with cup marks

Mousterian level

Stratigraphic section AB

C

Stratigraphic section CD

A

B

D

Edges of the cup-marked block

Edges of the pit

Plan and stratigraphic section of the pit where the Mousterian child was buried.
1. Skull.
2. Skeleton.

he must therefore have been taken care of by his tribe: Neanderthalers had no experience of exclusion. Finally, the deliberate burying of the individuals is indisputable, except for the last discovery, strongly cryoturbated. The funerary structure generally consists of a pit, sometimes completed with small stone slabs or a mound of earth. The depositing of offerings is suggested by the presence of some fine flint tools or a finely incised bone. In one case, the rites seem to have been complex: the three-year-old child of burial VI may have been decapitated post-mortem at La Ferrassie. Whatever the case, the pit was covered by a heavy limestone slab decorated with small cup marks

hollowed out of the stone. This type of evidence, however slight and difficult to interpret, bears witness to the Neanderthalers' "religiosity" and represents the first traces of spirituality before the blossoming of early artistic or symbolic expressions attributed to *Homo sapiens sapiens* (Cro-Magnon).

Endscrapers on blades, 12.3 cm for the largest.

Whether one agrees or not with that interpretation, these signs must have had great symbolic value for these first modern humans. Other Aurignacian dwellings within a radius of fifteen kilometres around Les Eyzies have yielded fine examples of these probable ethnic markers, covering a period of nearly 5,000 years. Among the most significant, those of Abri du Poisson, Gorge d'Enfer, denote a strong Aurignacian occupation over 30,000 years ago.

Spear point, bone, with split base.

Cup marks and female sexual symbols.

Cup marks and engravings.

Female sexual symbol.

In this respect, the contribution of La Ferrassie is still crucial: the Aurignacian art on blocks dug up on the site is among the earliest known symbolic expressions in the world.

Whether they were really mobiliary art, or whether on the contrary they are due to the partial collapse of the wall, fossilised in the occupation levels, these blocks generally associate several ornamental techniques. Many were given a regular shape, then often engraved, delicately or more coarsely with blows from a flint pick whose successive impacts give the impression of a deep continuous incision. Painting (in red ochre) is also attested, although more rarely, as is the decoration consisting of juxtaposed cup marks already glimpsed during the Mousterian period. At least thirty decorated pieces have been found in all the Aurignacian levels at La Ferrassie. The themes recorded have become classical: sketchy animal figures (felines, caprids, equids, and a few indeterminate animals) and more or less complex signs, from the simple cup mark to the strongly incised triangle, sufficiently suggestive to evoke female genitalia.

Abri du Poisson, Gorge d'Enfer: hunters, gatherers, and fishermen

The initial history of this site, also called "Val d'Enfer" ("Hell Valley"), merges with that of the early days of prehistoric research in the Vézère region, the work of Lartet and his patron Christy in 1863–4. The encounter between man and sites was symbolic:

Lartet gave his name to one of the shelters and the picturesque term of *Val infernalien* was for a time eponymous for a chronological and cultural period, later known by a different name. Modern humans seem to have been the first to frequent this deep valley

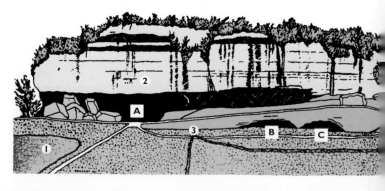

regularly, in particular the large shelter (1,600 square metres), but medieval occupation and the establishment of a saltpetre quarry during the Revolutionary period have of course deleted all trace of their visits.

The small "Lartet" shelter, filled in to a large extent, was intact in 1863. Apart from a few traces of the Châtelperronian, it mainly yielded typically Aurignacian material, including enigmatic pieces of bone covered with small cup marks—a lunar calendar according

to Marshack—and numerous painted limestone plaquettes, the remains of a since collapsed roof once entirely covered in red ochre.

Moving towards the end of the valley, the cave-shelter called "des Yeuses" or "Oreille d'Enfer" ("Hell's Ear") comes into sight, slightly set back. Its occupation levels seem to be more recent, Solutrean and especially Perigordian (Gravettian) if the attributions established on the basis of the abundant finds dug up most anarchically between 1860 and 1940 can be believed. Extending out from the gallery into the porch, the archaeological layers covered the animal engravings discovered by Massias in 1922, representing caprids or does, completed with a series of engraved

Grand Abri Lartet and Abri Lartet. Abri du Poisson (inset).

Locations of the shelters, on the left side of Gorge d'Enfer.
A. Grand Abri.
B. Abri Lartet.
C. Abri du Poisson.
D. Abri Pasquet.
1. Pond.
2. Lookout lodge.
3. Source.
4. D 47 road.
5. River Vézère.

cup marks made by picking at the rock and that suggest several carnivores' footprints. Some incisions and engraved lines as well as red signs, sticks, or dots, complete what remains of the decoration of this unpretentious but interesting site, listed as an historic monument in 1932.

Abri du Poisson remains the brightest gem of the parietal art of this magic spot. Literally adjoining Abri Lartet, but hidden by undergrowth and filled in to a large extent, this small cavity (eight by seven metres), glimpsed by Emile Rivière, was excavated "by chance" in 1892 by Louis Giraud, an amateur prehistorian who named it Gorge d'Enfer B. Two archaeological layers in front of the shelter, Aurignacian and Gravettian, were seriously damaged by Galou, the owner of the neighbouring café, in 1898. In 1912 Giraud resumed excavations of the Aurignacian layer at the base, with no very interesting results, at least for science.

Engraved vulva, Abri du Poisson.

Engraving on reindeer antler, interpreted as a lunar calendar and discovered by Lartet and Christy in 1865, 10 cm long, Upper Palaeolithic, Aurignacian, Abri Lartet.

That same year a local man called Jean Marsan, but with the predestined nickname "Jean le Pêcheur" ("John the Fisherman"), discovered the sculpture whose fame immediately spread outside France. Dr Schukard of the Berlin Anthropological Museum commissioned, perhaps in relation with Otto Hauser, its attempted removal from the wall: the marks are still clearly visible. This reprehensible undertaking fortunately failed

thanks to Denis Peyrony's energetic intervention: the shelter was purchased by the French government on 29 March 1913, and its scheduling as an historic monument may represent the first application of the law of 1913. From 1917, Peyrony was responsible for the maintenance of the site. Soon the rather overly energetic washing down of the roof, in preparation for the construction of a wall to close the cavity, provided an opportunity to resume excavations, mainly limited to exploiting the old spoil heaps.

The earliest occupation dates back to the Typical Aurignacian, confirmed by the abundant material collected: remains of cold-climate fauna (reindeer, horse, mammoth, musk ox), lithic tools very similar to the series from Abri Lartet—probably and logically synonymous with a synchronous occupation of both sites—and, above all, bone implements (split-based spears, a fine incised smoothing implement, and a remarkable *bâton percé* with a spiral groove).

Even more remarkable are the numerous remains bearing witness to a parietal decoration attributable to that period: engravings on blocks of stone, such as a vulva very similar to those found at Blanchard and Castanet (Castel Merle, near Sergeac) or La Ferrassie, the forequarters of a deer reminiscent of the art of Pair-non-Pair or La Croze-à-Gontran, various rock flakes, and an imposing limestone slab (still *in situ*) depicting cervids and caprids, executed in sunken relief and cut-away engraving. To all that must be added 107 fragments of the painted roof, the subject of recent, as yet unpublished, research. Thirty thousand years ago, Abri du Poisson must certainly have been a fine sanctuary with a rich decoration coloured with various types of red pigments and black manganese paint: proof that the roof, before its deterioration, was bicoloured—unexpected for that period but which

Carved and engraved salmon in Abri du Poisson, 1.05 m long.

has recently been confirmed by the Gravettian paintings discovered in Grotte Chauvet (Vallon-Pont-d'Arc, Ardèche). The second occupation phase of the shelter is fossilised in the upper layer, which has yielded a small lithic series typical of the Gravettian (around 25,000 years ago) with Noailles burins, Gravette points, and classical flechettes (small foliate points, sometimes called Bayac points). Before considering the famous sculpture of a salmon that occupies the centre of the cavity, it is time for some contemporary history. While a questionable engraving of a horse observed by Max Sarradet in 1975 should be viewed with caution, a negative hand print discovered in December of the same year and miraculously preserved in spite of the washing down of the roof on 5 September 1918 is indisputably genuine. In comparison with equivalent decorations widespread in the Pyrenean caves, where they have been radiocarbon-dated to 26,000–27,000 BP[*], these apparently modest vestiges represent the second strong argument in favour of attributing the salmon to the Upper Perigordian, after that of the ice damage, of course. Created by a technique similar to sunk or hollow relief or cut-away engraving— in which all the carving lies within a hollowed-out area below the surface plane— the kelt (salmon after spawning) is depicted life-size (1.05 metres long). It is decorated with a long tapered motif from its anus to its gills, perhaps evoking

the reproductive organs, egg-filled ovaries, or the soft roe pouch. Two rings have been carved at the level of the caudal fin, while the dorsal fin seems to have been replaced by a rectangular sign bearing seven incisions, thus conferring a certain ambiguity on the figure. This central work of art was not isolated: a few poorly preserved engravings, cup marks (fairly comparable with those at Oreille d'Enfer), the remains of a broad expanse of red ochre covering the whole of the roof, several black lines, and seven rings together with a fishhook-shaped sign reveal the scattered remains of what must have been a rich decoration, setting off the salmon. An obvious evocation of the aquatic world and the earliest depiction of a fish known anywhere in the world, this theme (rare moreover in parietal art) confirms our ancestors' interest in fishing as far back as 25,000 years ago; it modifies the usual image of simple reindeer hunters. Close to the river, in the immediate vicinity of a ford, Abri du Poisson was perhaps a sanctuary for seasonal fishermen, complementing their usual food resources by a specialised activity particularly profitable in the spawning season. Thus, the notion of a population in close symbiosis with the environment, capable of making full use of it, and accordingly drawing up a calendar of annual subsistence activities, gradually emerges— some 10,000 years before the classical Magdalenian period.

[*]*BP:*
Before present, indicating in fact dates prior to AD 1950, the conventional "present", when the radiocarbon dating method was established.

Laugerie-Haute, print from *La Création de l'homme* by Henri du Cleuziou, 1887.

Laugerie-Haute: thousands of years of occupation

Relatively unknown by the general public, this huge rockshelter, over 200 metres long and 30 or 40 metres wide during prehistoric times, exploits to the full its jumble of huge blocks, presenting visitors with a grandiose mystery-filled space.

From outside, however, it has such a discreet appearance that it is not even an eponym site. Since the earliest research, carried out at the time of roadworks along the Vézère, Laugerie-Haute has represented a "complete" site for prehistorians, liberally referred to whatever the speciality: parietal art, mobiliary art, stratigraphy, burials, dwelling structures, cultural transitions, etc. With its neighbour, Laugerie-Basse, famous for its mobiliary art (only about ten metres downstream), the sequence of the two Laugerie shelters provides a rare stratigraphic continuity, covering with practically no gaps twenty-five millennia of human occupation, from the Upper Palaeolithic to the Gallo-Roman period, and even modern times, judging by the age of the house, presumed to be from the seventeenth century, which seals off the sequence and protects the archaeological reserve established in the centre of the site. Monopolised by Hauser, who lived on the spot and installed a "sales counter of finds" there, the site benefited from early twentieth-century patriotism. The antiquary left the region for the last time one evening in August 1914, leaving the site in a state close to its present aspect, very different from its original condition: the huge slope set against the cliff, whence emerged the great rocks, marking a former rock porch,

had been replaced by two huge excavations that—put into shape by other archaeologists—would become Laugerie-Haute East and Laugerie-Haute West. During the 1920s Peyrony resumed more meticulous excavations after having cleared 2,000 cubic metres of spoil, and found major objects, which had survived the disaster. His results, published in 1938, established the stratigraphy, the general outline of which is still valid. Certain levels correspond to complex periods, concerning, depending on the age, the Late Aurignacian (V) or Late Gravettian with characteristics bordering on the Magdalenian, whence the name "Proto-Magdalenian". Worthy of note also, the whole of the Solutrean sequence, "the Laugerian", framed by transitional episodes laying the foundations of impassioned and unfinished scientific debates, in particular on the origin and legacy of this brilliant civilisation. A few decades later François Bordes contributed new arguments: he carried out meticulous excavations, identifying in the sequence at least forty-two individual layers, twenty-eight of which contained finds, often separated by a sterile border, and attempted to define a cultural micro-evolution based on a statistico-typological study of the lithic industry (the famous "Bordes method"). At the same time, he discovered some rare but important works of art: a magnificent feline, the only piece truly attributable to the Early Solutrean, and a decorated block bearing polychrome traces dating from the Middle Gravettian.

Panorama of the cliffs along the Vézère between Gorge d'Enfer and Laugerie.
A. Gorge d'Enfer.
B. Laugerie-Basse.
C. Laugerie-Haute.

Publicity for Otto Hauser's excavations at Laugerie-Haute, in French, German, and English.

FOUILLES DE O. HAUSER
LES EYZIES
DORDOGNE (FRANCE)

LAUGERIE HAUTE (Les Eyzies)

LAUGERIE HAUTE (LES EYZIES)
BUREAU DER AUSGRABUNGSLEITUNG
Ausstellung prähistorischer Funde.
· PLÄNE · PHOTOGRAPHIEN ·
Wagen, Gute Zimmer, Angenehmer Aufenthalt,
DUNKELKAMMER

Bureau de la Direction des Fouilles préhistoriques.
ACHEULLÉEN, MOUSTÉRIEN, AURIGNACIEN,
SOLUTRÉEN, MAGDALÉNIEN.
Exposition des objets préhistoriques, Plans, Photographies
VOITURES, CHAMBRES, SÉJOUR AGRÉABLE
CHAMBRE NOIRE

LAUGERIE HAUTE (LES EYZIES)
Prehistoric excavations Manager's office.
· EXHIBITION OF PREHISTORIC OBJETS ·
· PLANS · PHOTOS ·
Carriages, Rooms to let. Agreable sejourn.
· DARK ROOM ·

**Overall view
of the site.**

Yet other archaeologists
excavating Laugerie-Haute
attempted, with mixed results,
to approach the domains
of palaeoethnology and
the palaeoenvironment.
François Bordes, moreover,
was not mistaken: in spite
of a series of generally
coherent radiocarbon dates,
between 18,300 and 13,850 BP
for the Magdalenian period
broadly speaking, he did not
exclude the possibility
that some layers or

occupation levels may have
been mixed, thus rendering
certain hypotheses illusory
or misleading. That made
consideration of the genesis
of the sedimentary deposits
indispensable, as it is an issue
affecting the reliability of any
interpretation. Results recently
proposed by Jean-Pierre Texier
indicate that the strata were
set in place by solifluction up
to and including the Upper
Solutrean. Above them,
for the Magdalenian,

Stratigraphic sections on the site.

the stratified aspect with segregation and open shingly levels points to a solifluction gulley with a stony front. The imposing blocks whose fall was thought to have put an end to the occupation of the shelter during the Middle Magdalenian would in fact, in view of the apparent absence of crushing patterns in the sediment, have been in place prior to the deposit of the archaeological layers. So should Laugerie-Haute be denied the scientific importance subscribed to by generations of archaeologists?

The answer is, of course, no. The reassessment of the site by means of the most modern methods of investigation clearly demonstrates both its weak and strong points. When its mode of sedimentation is taken into account, this shelter obviously cannot answer certain palaeoethnographic or spatial questions. On the other hand, it remains an extensive scientific reservoir, a source for further research, even if the issue of its time scale, and above all of its micro-chronological evolution, is indeed illusory.

The west side of the site, simplified transversal and longitudinal stratigraphic sections (after Peyrony)

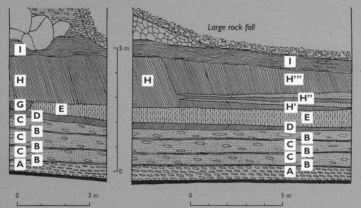

A Rocky ground and sterile limestone scree.

B Gravettian (Upper Perigordian).

C Sterile scree layer.

D Late Aurignacian (V).

E Sterile layer.

G Peyrony's Early Solutrean or Proto-Solutrean (mixture).

H' Lower Solutrean, with large laurel leaves.

H'' Middle Solutrean, with shouldered points (layers containing numerous artefacts).

H''' Upper and Late Solutrean.

I Early Magdalenian, Middle and Upper Magdalenian (traces), and Azilian (east side only).

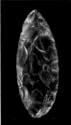

Bovid, detail.

Shouldered point.

Flat-faced point.

Ovibos (musk ox) head, Solutrean (Saint-Germain-en-Laye, Musée des Antiquités nationales).

Plaquette known as "Woman and reindeer", engraving on reindeer antler, Laugerie-Basse, Magdalenian (Saint-Germain-en-Laye, Musée des Antiquités nationales).

Abri Pataud: a site museum and laboratory

The property of the Muséum national d'histoire naturelle, Paris, this prehistoric site lies in the heart of Les Eyzies-de-Tayac, halfway between the famous Cro-Magnon shelter (250 m upstream) and the Musée national de Préhistoire.

Proto-Magdalenian skull from Abri Pataud.

Discovered in the late nineteenth century by its owner, Martial Pataud, this shelter was the subject of several limited excavations before being investigated on a large scale (from 1958 to 1964) by a team led by Professor Hallam Movius, Jr. of Harvard University and the Peabody Museum. It proved to be one of the great sites in Périgord thanks to its abundant archaeological material and interesting stratigraphy.

Its fill was mainly due to the gradual collapse of one or several overhanging rock canopies during the first half of the Upper Palaeolithic. The stratigraphy consists of fourteen main prehistoric occupation levels following one another to a depth of 9.25 metres.

The nine lowest layers correspond to the Aurignacian. The middle of the sequence includes four Gravettian levels, and the last occupation dates from the Solutrean. In addition, the last phase of the Gravettian has yielded numerous very well-preserved human remains.

Apart from the human remains, now in the Musée de l'Homme, Paris, all the archaeological material found during the excavations has been kept on site. The Abri Pataud collections represent a reference for *Homo sapiens sapiens* cultures during the first half of the Upper Palaeolithic in south-western France. The property also includes a second uncollapsed rockshelter, slightly above Abri Pataud.

A museum, inaugurated in 1990, is open to visitors almost year round, as is the prehistoric site. An important archaeological stratigraphic section is preserved as reference around the last excavation. University research work is still being undertaken on the collections, some of which are yet to be published. They provide help in improving our understanding of the subsistence behaviour, technology, and symbolic aspects of the Palaeolithic occupants of Abri Pataud. The site also serves as a reception centre for field training organised by the prehistory department of the Muséum national d'histoire naturelle, Paris, and a training site for laboratory techniques (classification, inventory, study) for students in prehistoric archaeology. Full-time archaeologists, researchers, and students preparing their doctoral thesis work in the reserves, as do French and foreign students on study assignments. The museum proposes courses for the public: initiation in excavation techniques, reconstructing palaeoenvironments and ways of life. Various activities set off the research work on the collections.

View of the museum and reserves.

Gravettian blades in the Abri Pataud museum.

Font-de-Gaume: a festival of polychrome decoration

This cave, on the left bank of the Beune Valley, less than a kilometre east of the village centre of Les Eyzies, is reached from the ticket office by a path running 400 metres along a high ledge overhanging a dry valley. Its porch and galleries were frequented during modern times, as various graffiti testify. The prehistoric works were revealed officially in September 1901, a few days after those of Les Combarelles, by Dr Louis Capitan, Abbé Henri Breuil, and Denis Peyrony, thus providing decisive arguments in favour of the recognition of this art. In the late nineteenth century, at the time of the discovery of the paintings in the famous Altamira Cave in Spain, and Pair-non-Pair, Gironde, and La Mouthe at Les Eyzies in France, controversy had arisen regarding the age of these works. The cave consists of a 120-metre-long main gallery hollowed out of the Coniacian◆ limestone, following a diaclasis◆ punctuated by several narrower sections where three side galleries and several small, often impassable, passages branch out. The first excavations were mainly carried out to allow progress through the cavity, soon opened to visitors and even provided with electric lighting in 1910.

◆**Coniacian:**
Geological limestone stage of the Secondary Era, Upper Cretaceous (about 75 million years ago).

◆**Diaclasis:**
A fracture or break without any displacement of the rock.

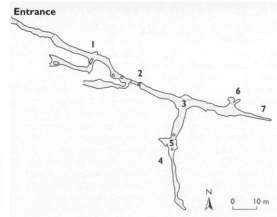

Entrance

1
2
6
3
7
5
4

N
0   10 m

Plan of the cave.
1. "Crossroads of the two entrances".
2. The "Rubicon".
3. "Large crossroads".
4. Side gallery.
5. The "Stalagmite Hall".
6. The "Bison Chamber".
7. End gallery.

According to palaeontological studies carried out between 1958 and 1964 in a side gallery, the cave was occupied by Mousterians, then by Châtelperronians, perhaps during the Solutrean and Magdalenian periods, and, finally, during the Bronze Age. The works of art date from the Early and Middle Magdalenian and even, for some, from the Solutrean. Over 200 painted or engraved figures, organised into compositions, occupy the four main sectors

The black frieze of cervids and caprids.

Bison with red horns.

Right-hand page, top to bottom and left to right
Two bison facing each other, bison, deer, bison and tectiform signs, two reindeer facing each other, rhinoceros, horse, wolf, reindeer, drawings by Henri Breuil, 1901–6.

of the network, separated by irregularities in the cave's morphology. While engravings have recently been recognised near the entrance, the first significant painted works only appear sixty metres further on, after a narrow passage nicknamed "the Rubicon". The animal and non-figurative decorations are some of humanity's greatest masterpieces. The inventory includes horses, cervids, mammoths, a rhinoceros, a few human figures, always stylised, and eighty-four bison. The non-figurative themes include tectiforms (i.e. roof-shaped signs), characteristic of Périgord,

which seem to establish a link with Les Combarelles, Bernifal, and Rouffignac. In the central sector of the cave a remarkable frieze of bison is superimposed, for several dozen metres, on a line of mammoths. Reindeer occupy a privileged position in certain conspicuous spots of the frieze. The cave has suffered from the ravages of time and from too many tourists over several decades. It is now strictly monitored: only a limited number of visitors are allowed to enter what is one of the finest sanctuaries of the late Palaeolithic era. Font-de-Gaume and Lascaux are two of the few caves containing polychrome paintings.

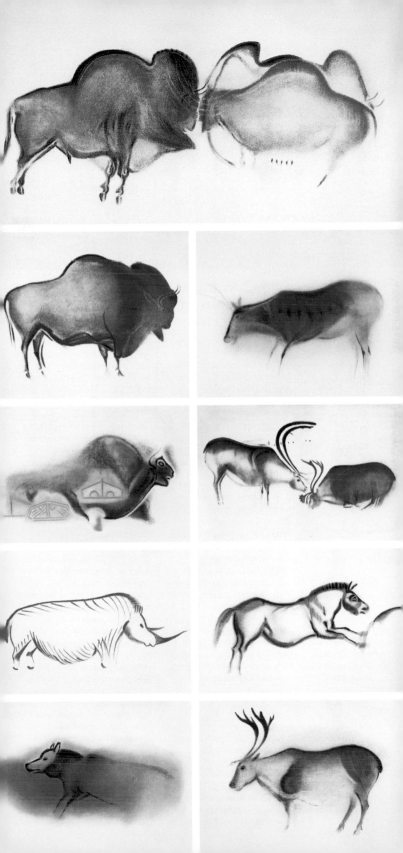

Les Combarelles: a profusion of engravings

◆**Couze/Lalinde type:** *A type of schematically engraved female figure seen in profile.*

With over 800 wall representations, for the most part engraved, the cave of Les Combarelles and its continuation, Les Combarelles II, are rightly considered two of the prime sanctuaries of the Magdalenian culture. The cave opening is less than three kilometres east of Les Eyzies on the edge of the D47 road, in a small eponym valley. Beyond a porch excavated by Rivière in 1892 two diverging galleries, called "Combarelles I" and "Combarelles II", plunge into the cliff. M. Berniche, the owner, informed Abbé Breuil, Louis Capitan, and Denis Peyrony that there were "beasts" on the walls. On 8 September 1901 they explored the first cavity: it is a long, narrow, and low-ceilinged zigzagging corridor (one metre wide by two metres at its highest points). They recognised

Reindeer facing each other, drawings by Henri Breuil.

hundreds of animal engravings. Abbé Breuil made drawings of them in 1924. More meticulous research was undertaken by Professor Claude Barrière from 1978 and has recently been published.

The decoration begins 70 metres from the entrance and is mainly concentrated in the last 160 metres before gradually disappearing in the section of the gallery that joins up with the network still in activity. Distributed on either side of the corridor, the works are finely incised (apart from a few black drawings) and depict a highly diversified fauna, organised in more or less crowded groups. Deciphering the horses, bison, aurochs, bears, reindeer, mammoths, lions, ibex, deer, wolves, rhinoceros, foxes, fish, etc., with their extremely tangled outlines, is facilitated by the frequently realistic treatment of the animals, which differentiates them from the numerous schematic, even stereotyped, anthropomorphic figures that are sometimes difficult to interpret. In addition these panels bear engraved signs with rows of sticks and tectiforms reminiscent of those of Bernifal, Font-de-Gaume, and Rouffignac.

Two stylistic phases have been identified at Les Combarelles: Middle and Late Magdalenian.

The latter culture is characterised by small female figures of the Couze/Lalinde◆ type, with schematic profiles, found throughout Europe at the same period and pointing to a true transcontinental cultural unity. These chronological attributions have been corroborated by two radiocarbon dates obtained from bone artefacts found in 1973 during rescue excavations under the entrance porch. The earliest occupation level dates from 13,680 (± 210) BP,

the upper level, for its part, is 2,000 years more recent (11,380 [± 210] BP). In order to respect conservation obligations, only a privileged public has the right to enter Les Combarelles I, in groups of six; it is one of the richest Magdalenian sanctuaries. Discovered in 1909 by M. Pomarel, the owner's son-in-law, Les Combarelles II is only open to researchers, by appointment. It contains engravings, including a remarkable and rare image of a saiga antelope.

Mammoth
drawn by Capitan on a letter telling of the discovery of Les Combarelles, 18 September 1901.

Female figures
engraved at Couze/Lalinde (top) and Les Combarelles (bottom).

The "falling cow" frieze, with a quadrangular sign and horses, axial gallery.

Lascaux: "the Sistine Chapel of prehistory"

The discovery of this cave by four teenagers in 1940 attracted such attention that even the tragic events of the time were overshadowed. The most recent study of the decoration, carried out by Norbert Aujoulat, attests to the huge quantity of art, with a total tally of 1,963 representations: 915 animals, 434 signs, 613 "indeterminate", and only one human being. This corresponds to nearly a seventh of all the parietal art known in France. The artists at Lascaux seem to have wished to stake their claim to the whole of the underground area, including the farthest sectors. This indicates an intention to transform the place into a sanctuary, confirmed by the large number and high quality of the lithic and bone artefacts. As far as the graphic aspect is concerned, the extremely contrasted state of the walls and ceilings led to the use of a variety of techniques. For example, the softest supports did not allow any corrections by the artists. In certain cases, the option chosen depended on whether the walls could be reached by scaffolding, or more simply by brushes fixed on the end of long wooden poles, leading for example to lines composed of a series of strokes painted side by side. Certain graphic inventions attain an exceptional level of perfection, like the third dimension which is expressed by the use of natural relief but also by the technique of limbs "in reserve" (i.e. left the original colour of the support or background). By deliberately deforming the image, the artists have even sometimes suggested the idea of depth. The inventory is dominated by horses (364 examples), followed by cervids (90).

Bovids, on the other hand, are rare (twenty-eight aurochs), bison are restricted to the ends of the cavity, and there are few carnivores. Examination of the friezes and compositions suggests that these artistic groups were created on a single occasion. A specific study devoted to the figures of horses shows that the image is constructed of various elements set in place in an invariable order: the mane, then flanks, neck, and withers by the projection of pigments, followed by the contours and anatomical details executed in drawing or engraving depending on the type of support. Study of the superimpositions on a given panel shows a standard chronological

"Chinese" horses, axial gallery.

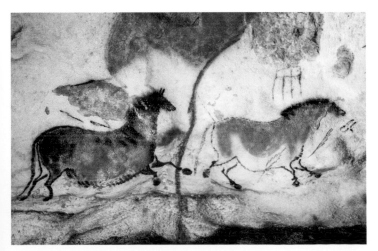

Two bison back to back, nave.

Black bull in front of a red cow, left wall of the Hall of Bulls.

construction: the horse was depicted first, then the aurochs, and finally the cervids. These animals are each portrayed with characteristics suggesting a certain seasonal aspect: the horse has its late winter or early spring coat, the aurochs is more evocative of the summer, while the cervids recall the autumn, each season probably bearing witness to a biological cycle indicating the start of mating. This "animal ritual" at the origin of life and the survival of the group reinforces the unity of the sanctuary of Lascaux where intense artistic activity seems to have flourished, perhaps limited to a single generation. Classically attributed to the Early Magdalenian, a new radiocarbon date (18,600 BP) has just been obtained for the cave from a mobiliary object. This places it in the Solutro-Magdalenian group, maintaining the Solutrean tradition while already heralding the great parietal art developments of the Magdalenian.

Tourism at Lascaux began in July 1948. The crowds of visitors and over-strong lighting led to the development of green algae and calcite deposits. In an attempt to return to a biological and climatic equilibrium, the cave was closed in 1963 and the public no longer admitted. A high-quality facsimile, called "Lascaux II", was opened nearby in 1983, allowing the many visitors to admire an accurate re-creation of the principal works of art.

Deer frieze,
right wall
of the nave.

*Following
double page*
**"The Scene
in the Shaft",**
at the back
of the apse.
A hunter and
a bison wounded
by a spear.

**Pink sandstone
lamp.**

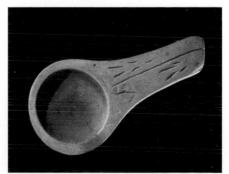

Grotte de la Mairie, Teyjat: the end of the ice age

Off the beaten track, this cave, little known to the general public, is of capital importance to Quaternary art. The original and joint initiative of the local authorities and the Centre des monuments nationaux has led to the creation of a museum area named after the man, Pierre Bourrinet, who discovered the engravings in 1903. Near the cave, it provides an indispensable complement to the visit of the original works of art by explaining the archaeological, environmental, and cultural context of the engraved animals, a particularly important aspect as this cave seems to be one of the few sites in France dating from the very end of the ice age. The animals depicted clearly convey the great climatic and environmental changes which, some 10,000 years ago, modified the way of life of the prehistoric hunter-gatherers and allowed the emergence of specific local cultural features. In the heart of the village, the cave owes its name to the late nineteenth-century construction of the former local administration building (now the "museum"). It fell to Denis Peyrony and the village schoolmaster,

Pierre Bourrinet, to authenticate the engraved decoration which, almost twenty years earlier, had escaped the attention of Périer du Carne. The variety of sources of supply for archaeological artefacts found in the cave—flint from Charente and the Bergerac region, jasper

from Nontron—reflects a remarkable phenomenon of contacts, bearing witness to communication routes between the foothills of the Massif Central and the hills of Périgord and Charente. Despite its very gentle relief the region

The museum, Teyjat.

was apparently not densely occupied, perhaps due to the fact that cliffs, caves, and rockshelters are few and far between. This adds to the interest of the sanctuary of La Mairie, especially as the evocation of the artefacts dug up in the nearby Abri Mège allows its context and role to be better understood. Both sites clearly belong to the same partially blocked karstic network.

The cave contained two strata dating to the Late Magdalenian (V and VI) in a scree cone measuring four metres at the entrance and narrowing to a mere twenty centimetres near the stalagmitic cascade.

The most frequently hunted and consumed animals reflect the beginning of the end of the Ice age. Apart from reindeer, relatively cold-climate, steppe-dwelling herbivores such as the horse are associated with more temperate species like red deer and wild boar. According to palaeontologists, cold-climate fauna continued to live on the borders of the Massif Central, but temperate species gradually moved into the completely altered landscapes: the open steppe-like horizons were being replaced by a denser, more enclosed forest environment, where pine predominated, accompanied by alder, birch, willow, oak, juniper, and elm.

The space available thus shrank due to new natural barriers (forests, permanent rivers and streams, etc.), a situation which, in conjunction with an apparent increase in population throughout south-western France, was to have considerable consequences. The last hunters were obliged to find new ways of managing natural resources. The broader range of food choices is obvious: small game, for example, was no longer neglected.

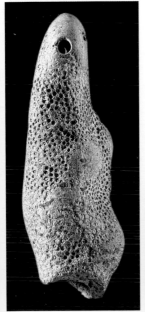

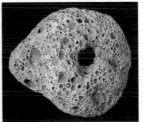

Ornaments and pendants made from fossils.

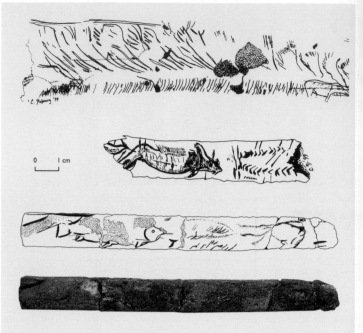

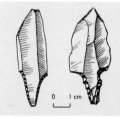

Top to bottom
Herd of reindeer
engraved on
an eagle's bone,
drawing.
**Seal and
chevrons
(herringbone
pattern),**
drawing.
Fish, drawing
and photograph,
engraved antler.
"Teyjat" point,
after D. de
Sonneville-Bordes.

Next page
**Engraved
animals.**

♦*Enveloping
limestone:*
*The stone forming
the geological
environment.*

Similarly, there was greater exploitation of the resources provided by rivers: the remains of fish have been found in profusion at Pont-d'Ambon, another site of the same period, alongside remains of deer and rabbit.
At Teyjat, a pronged harpoon made of bone and examples of mobiliary art reflect this trend: an antler "wedge" bears an engraved salmon, and a half-round antler rod a very realistic seal.
The traditional Upper Palaeolithic common lithic "tool kit" (endscrapers, burins, blade-based tools, etc.) was complemented by retouched points with a short tang, called "Teyjat points", very similar to the projectile points found in Northern Europe (Hamburg, Lingby), good "markers" for the Late Magdalenian.
Some of the bone tools stand out by their exceptional size—one projectile point even reaches the length of 370 millimetres— or carved decoration, bordering on mobiliary art, like the ornaments made from seashells or fossils, reaching a peak

with two jet (lignite) pendants carved in the round with two horses' heads.
As far as mobiliary art is concerned, important examples include an eagle's cubitus engraved with a herd of stylised reindeer, a rod decorated with deer heads where dots may

perhaps symbolise their coats, and the famous antler *bâton percé* from Mège associating a doe, a horse, large birds, eels or serpentiform figures, and a few part animal-part human figures, like imps with chamois heads which, when they were discovered, were assimilated, perhaps rather too rapidly, with the Australian fertility gods known as *ratapas*.
With regard to parietal art, the local context was not very favourable: the enveloping limestone♦ is totally unsuitable

Engraved panels, drawings by Henri Breuil.

for engraving, so the artists had no choice but to accept, in a zone poorly lit by daylight, the technical constraints of a stalagmitic cascade in amber-coloured calcite, a very hard material to engrave with flint tools and allowing no alterations. Recorded by Henri Breuil and Claude Barrière, and more recently studied by Norbert Aujoulat, the decoration mainly consists of animals. The total absence of signs and human depictions is indeed an original feature of the cavity. In addition, the 48 images, distributed over seven panels still *in situ* and a few isolated blocks found during excavations, confirm their singularity. Far from being merely juxtaposed, the figures, including representations of young animals, are often associated in pairs. The majority of the figures represent reindeer, followed by red deer, bear, bison, horse, and aurochs, of extremely high quality. These species, from cold or more temperate climates, probably correspond to successive phases of engraving, as could be expected from the archaeological material discovered. The difficult engraving technique is here perfectly suited to the artists' wishes: while seeking out the volume of the stone surface, they demonstrate

0   1 cm

their concern with anatomical detail. They have managed to convey admirably behaviour, seasonality, even movement, attaining an unmatched degree of realism.

The obvious kinship with contemporary mobiliary art, with regard to technique, style, and themes, also appears in the miniaturisation of certain images (for example the small deer on the entrance slab). That sufficed for André Leroi-Gourhan to consider it the last stage of his stylistic chronology ("late style IVb"). Since then, in spite of some recent discoveries, Ice age art still culminates at Teyjat before disappearing forever. It was the end of one world and the start of the development of new societies of producers, farmers, stock-breeders, often relatively sedentary and builders of villages and megalithic monuments, which are not unknown in Périgord.

Heads of cervids and chevrons engraved on antler, photographs and drawings.

Harpoon (fragment).

Rhinoceros drawn in black oxide of manganese.

♦**Campanian:**
An Upper Cretaceous chalky limestone level, belonging to the Secondary era (dating from 75–70 million years ago).

♦**Santonian:**
An Upper Cretaceous chalky limestone level, belonging to the Secondary era (dating from 80–75 million years ago).

♦**Sauveterrian:**
The name given in 1928 to designate a culture following the Magdalenian, characterised by its abundant microlithic industries (between approximately 9500 and 7500 BC).

Rouffignac:
the cave of a hundred mammoths

The cave of Rouffignac, Dordogne, also called the "Miremont" cave, was formed at the point of contact of the Campanian♦ and Santonian♦ cretaceous limestone, half-way up the right slope of the Labinche Valley. This huge cave contains a network of nearly ten kilometres, spread over three levels. The upper network, the richest in parietal art, begins after the entrance by a vast corridor about eight metres in diameter, which branches out all along its length of around one kilometre. The discovery of the cave in 1956 by Romain Robert and Louis-René Nougier sparked off the "war of the mammoths", a heated scientific debate regarding the authenticity of these parietal decorations, all the more surprising in that François de Belle-Forest had already observed, around 1575, various figures of "beasts", unidentifiable

at the time. According to the most recent excavations, its porch contains seven post-Palaeolithic occupation levels, from the Sauveterrian♦ to the Middle Ages. More than 250 representations have been inventoried, with a majority of animal themes. The mammoth dominates, with over 150 depictions, accompanied by bison, horses, ibex, rhinoceros, a carnivore (bear?), and a fairly realistic serpentiform, as well as a few anthropomorphic figures, occasionally composite. Abstract representations are also found, with tectiforms and "apostrophes" and "macaroni" made by drawing fingers along soft surfaces—but no sexual symbols—allowing an age of around 13,000–14,000 BP to be proposed. The whole of the decoration seems to have been conceived at once, although a few later additions cannot be ruled out.

The themes are typical of Franco-Cantabrian art, even if the number of rhinoceros and especially of mammoths is surprising. The techniques differ depending on the—extremely variable—state of the support: engraving with flint burins on the zones hardened by calcite, or finger tracings in the soft areas. Both techniques may be combined within a single animal figure, always subject to the same graphic framework and enhanced with very realistic anatomical details such as the mammoth's anal flap. The colour is fairly uniform, restricted to a very few red lines made with clay and, especially, to the black drawings executed with manganese oxide. The style is homogeneous; it seems reduced to essentials, spontaneous and efficient, with strokes engraved in a single movement, implying a technique perfectly mastered by specialists. At Rouffignac the mammoth obviously seems to have played a fundamental role in the Palaeolithic population's beliefs. It is constantly associated with finger tracings. Apart from a few isolated drawings, the animals are grouped, facing each other or in friezes, and bear witness to an organised form of graphic expression: only some galleries have been decorated, together with the sinkholes giving access to the various small side passages. Important restoration work was carried out in the cave between 1990 and 1994 in order to remove graffiti dating from modern times.

Mammoth incised in the limestone.

Horse carved in high relief.

Abri du Cap-Blanc

Listed as an historic monument in 1926, this shelter is set in a Coniacian limestone outcrop on the right bank of the Grande Beune (municipality of Marquay), a few kilometres east of Les Eyzies. The first excavations, carried out by Peyrille on behalf of Dr Lalanne, began in 1909, resulting, in less than four months, in the uncovering of a carved frieze apparently resting on the base of the archaeological fill. Two years later a burial was discovered, rapidly exported to the Field Museum, Chicago. Other, smaller excavations took place: in 1930 under Denis Peyrony, and between 1963 and 1969 under Alain Roussot, curator of the Musée d'Aquitaine, Bordeaux. The shelter measures fifteen metres in length, thirteen of which are occupied by the animal sculptures: horses, bison, cervids, sometimes superimposed, were probably, like the whole of the wall, originally coloured with ochre, occasionally observed during the early excavations.

These were not particularly careful, and the lower register of the decoration was damaged, especially as the wall is fragile and the limestone badly eroded over several metres. The archaeological fill apparently consisted of two layers separated by a sterile level, attributable to the Middle and Upper Magdalenian, effectively corresponding to the early style IV of the sculptures. A protective wall, built in 1911 to prevent the proliferation of algae on the rock surface, means this "surface sanctuary" is bathed in a shadowy light, which has modified its general atmosphere. A small museum-lobby has been added. The verve and strong relief of the frieze, executed with a flint pick, make Cap-Blanc one of the greatest masterpieces of monumental sculpture in Quaternary art.

Partial view of the Cap-Blanc frieze.

Ruins of the castle at Les Eyzies, c. 1910.

Inauguration of the large museum gallery, 19 July 1931.

Musée national de Préhistoire

The Musée national de Préhistoire (National Museum of Prehistory) originated in a highly symbolic encounter between a young schoolmaster, Denis Peyrony, destined for a brilliant future as a prehistorian, and a ruined but still imposing castle set into a cliff occupied by human beings for tens of thousands of years. The science of prehistory already commanded respect thanks to numerous excavations and discoveries when Peyrony was recruited in 1911 by the Ministère des Beaux-Arts (Ministry for Fine Arts). He was responsible for ensuring the protection of the archaeological sites, and had the restoration of the castle of Les Eyzies begun in order to transform it into the future museum and archaeological storage facility. He even set the village on the path of cultural tourism by opening the decorated caves to the public in 1920.

Installation of the museum was interrupted by World War I, then continued with several phases: an official inauguration in 1923, completed by the erection of the symbolic statue of primitive man sculpted by Paul Dardé, inaugurated in 1931. Élie Peyrony, who continued his father's work after 1936, had to find a solution for dealing with the increased numbers of visitors and archaeologists, and the cramped premises. Two buildings were constructed in 1966–7, at the end of the terrace, against the cliffside; one served as the museum reserves, the other as a laboratory and room where archaeologists and researchers could work. Another reception area for the public was built near the former castle moat. The museum originally depended on the Direction régionale des Antiquités préhistoriques (regional prehistoric antiquities department) for Aquitaine,

Entrance of the Musée national de Préhistoire crowned by the castle of Les Eyzies, which housed the former museum.

but in 1972 it was placed under the Direction des Musées de France (the agency responsible for all museums in France). Jean Guichard, who had succeeded Élie Peyrony in 1967, undertook the complete renovation of the castle, completed in 1979, with the opening of the large gallery presenting the morpho-typology of lithic industries. In view of the ever-increasing number of visitors and the rapid progress of scientific research, in 1984 the Ministère de la Culture decided on a new extension. The museum has expanded its collaboration with the region's many research organisations (Centre national de préhistoire, Institut de préhistoire et de géologie du Quaternaire at Bordeaux University, etc.) and, over the past fifteen years, its collections have increased fivefold. It now contains series of worldwide interest in the fields of palaeontology, prehistory, palaeoanthropology, and art. Rescue excavations were carried out from 1989 to 1991 on the site of the future premises, where a prehistoric site was identified. The construction of the new buildings, designed by the architect Jean-Pierre Buffi, began in late 1995. With an additional surface of 5,000 square metres, including over 1,500 square metres of exhibition galleries, the world capital of prehistory is now equipped with the first structure specialised in prehistoric archaeology, in keeping with its reputation. The museum fulfils several functions in addition to presenting its collections to the general public: heritage conservation, the identification and evaluation of archaeological remains, participation in excavations, and scientific publications (periodicals, monographs). The research centre welcomes archaeologists and students from all over the world and collaborates with other institutions, both in France and abroad. Its laboratory includes in particular reference collections of animal bones, lithic industries, and palaeontological comparisons. A policy of producing replicas of original objects made under scientific supervision, aimed at studying and preserving stratigraphic sequences and dwelling structures, has been set in place. The museum collections include about 6 million objects, 18,000 of which are on display, recounting the 400,000 years of human presence in south-western France up to the end of the ice age.

The new museum layout

The circuit is based on various documentary supports and modern technologies—audio-visual methods, interactive consoles, replicas, and models— to provide information corresponding to the expectations of all visitors: children, adults, novices, or enthusiasts. Dermoplastic reconstructions of prehistoric people and long-extinct animals are also presented, taking into account the most recent scientific hypotheses. The visit begins with a dive into time, several million years ago. Visitors, walking along a corridor cut into the cliff, thus approach the issue of mankind's origins. Climbing a staircase topped with a light well, they move up the "well of time" and discover the routes by which Europe was populated, and the long tale of nearly 400,000 years of human presence in the Vézère Valley.

The "timeline"

At the start of the first museum gallery, in a section devoted to "keys for interpreting prehistoric times", visitors can familiarise themselves with dating methods used by archaeologists. They then follow the "timeline" along a display case presenting the evolution of the prehistoric populations' technologies and tools, and their environments.

Reconstruction of the adolescent known as "Nariokotome Boy", Lake Turkana, Kenya, and of **the Laetoli footprints,** Tanzania.

Grotte Vaufrey, couche X, fouilles J.-Ph. Rigaud

La Micoque, couche 4, fouilles D. Peyrony

Grotte Vaufrey, couche X, fouilles J.-Ph. Rigaud

...aufrey, couche XI supérieure, fouilles J.-Ph. Rigaud

The large display cabinet and the "timeline".

Overall view of the upper gallery.

Specific areas presenting numerous examples of archaeological evidence are devoted to the principal prehistoric periods: "Neanderthal times", "The appearance of modern mankind", and "The end of the ice age". At regular intervals the environment is brought to life by skeletons or reconstructions of animals. Lastly, a large model at the end of the gallery illustrates possible movements of the populations that inhabited the region.

The domestic area
On the upper floor, visitors have the impression of being in a dwelling that has just been abandoned by its occupants: various activity zones have been recreated with the help of artefacts placed in context and casts of archaeological ground surfaces illustrating the gathering of materials, fishing, hunting, hearths, etc. The circuit then examines symbolic aspects such as burial practices, personal ornaments, and mobiliary art, ending with an evocation of the underground sanctuaries.

A short bibliography

Bahn, Paul (ed.), *The New Penguin Dictionary of Archaeology* (Harmondsworth: Penguin, 2004).

Bahn, Paul and Vertut, Jean, *Journey through the Ice Age* (London: Weidenfeld & Nicolson, 1997).

Bordes, François, *Typologie du Paléolithique ancien et moyen* (Bordeaux: Éditions du CNRS, 1979–81).

Bosinski, Gerhard, *Les Civilisations de la préhistoire. Les chasseurs du paléolithique supérieur (-40 000 à -10 000 av. J.-C.)* (Paris: Errance, 1990).

Breuil, Henri, *Quatre cents siècles d'art pariétal* (Montignac: CEDP, 1952).

Cleyet-Merle, Jean-Jacques, *La Province préhistorique des Eyzies, 400 000 ans d'implantation humaine* (Paris: Éditions du CNRS, 1995).

Cunliffe, Barry (ed.), *The Oxford Illustrated Prehistory of Europe* (Oxford: Oxford University Press, 1994).

Gamble, Clive, *The Palaeolithic Settlement of Europe* (Cambridge: Cambridge University Press, 1986).

Jaubert, Jacques, *Chasseurs et artisans du Mousterian. Histoire de la France préhistorique de -25 000 ans à -30 000 ans* (Paris: La Maison des Roches, 1999).

L'Art des cavernes, atlas des grottes ornées paléolithiques françaises, preface by André Leroi-Gourhan (Paris: Ministère de la Culture, 1984).

Laville, Henry, Rigaud, Jean-Philippe, and Sackett, James, *Rock Shelters of the Périgord* (New York: Academic Press, 1980).

Leroi-Gourhan, André, *The Art of Prehistoric Man in Western Europe* (London: Thames & Hudson, 1968).

— *The Dawn of European Art* (Cambridge: Cambridge University Press, 1982).

McIntosh, Jane, *The Practical Archaeologist* (London: Thames & Hudson, 1999).

Tuffreau, Alain, *L'Acheuléen. De l'homo erectus à l'homme de Néandertal. Histoire de la France préhistorique de -600 000 ans à -250 000 ans* (Paris: La Maison des Roches, 2004).

Acknowledgements

Norbert Augoulat for his magnificent photographs; Jean Archambeau, Claude Barrière, Laurence Bourguignon, Brigitte and Gilles Delluc, Marie-Louise Gaussen, Jean-Michel Geneste, Roland Nespoulet, Jean Placard, and Jean-Philippe Rigaud for their collaboration regarding the illustrations.

Captions

CMN: Paris, Centre des monuments nationaux
MNP: Les Eyzies, musée national de Préhistoire
Cover
Front: Stag, Lascaux.
Back: see p. 14.
Front flap: see pp. 48–49b.
Visit p. 30: engraved panels in Grotte de la Mairie, Teyjat, drawings by H. Breuil.
Chronology
Left to right and top to bottom
• Prehistoric sites in the Vézère Valley and nearby: see pp. 31, 36, 40–41, 50, 46.
• Human evolution: see pp. 10, 13, skull of the Magdalenian adolescent from Roc de Cave, Saint-Cirq-de-Madelon, Lot (MNP-distri.RMN/Ph. Jugie).
• Technology: see pp. 11, 14, 16, 18, Font-Robert points, La Ferrassie, after D. de Sonneville-Bordes, 22, Magdalenian III spears, Laugerie-Haute.
• Art: see pp. 39tr, 43, 20, 49, 7.
• Climate: see pp. 17b, 22–23b.
• Fauna: drawings after André Leroi-Gourhan.

Photographic credits

All rights reserved: 8–9t, 27t, 28t, 29c and b, 65b, 69b, 70–71, 72, 73; J.-Cl. Blanchet: 8b, 9b, 33c; CMN/N. Aujoulat: inside front flap, 55; Brigitte and Gilles Delluc: 28b, 29h; MNP/collection: 5, 6b, 17, 22–23b, 26, 27c and b, 44c, 45b; MNP-distri. RMN: 57b, 64t and b, 65t, 66c, 67, 69t and b; MNP-distri. RMN/L. Hamon: 6t; MNP-distri. RMN/Ph. Jugie: 1t, 2–3, 4, 11b–13, 14b, 15, 18, 19, 21, 22t, 23t, 24, 25, 31, 33t, 35, 36, 38, 39, 42t, 46, 47t, 48t, 52–53, 56, 57t, 61b, 76–79; Paris, Musée de l'Homme/J. Oster: 50, 51; Périgueux, Centre national de préhistoire/Ministère de la Culture/N. Aujoulat: cover (front and back), 1b, 7t, 40–41t, 43, 44–45t, 54, 58–60, 62–63; Périgueux, Musée du Périgord: 4t; RMN/L. Hamon: outside front flap, 48–49b; RMN/J. Schormans: 49t; Tautavel, Centre européen de recherches préhistoriques: 10; Vertut: 1c, 20, 42b.

Series editor
Alix Sallé
Translator
Ann Sautier-Greening
Copy editor
Chrisoula Petridis
Graphic design
Atalante/Paris
Layout
Anne Chevry, Jean-François Gautier
Production coordinator
Carine Merse
Photoengraving
Scann'Ouest/Saint-Aignan-de-Grand-Lieu
Printing
Néo-Typo/Besançon, France

© Éditions du patrimoine, Centre des monuments nationaux Paris, 2005
Dépôt légal: December 2005
Reprinting: April 2008
ISSN: 1159-1722
ISBN: 978-2-85822-553-8